MW01486740

Global Voices
for
Peace

Susan Hartley

Global Voices
For
Peace

An Introduction to Peacebuilders and the Hope They Bring

Edited by Susan Hartley, Ph.D.

Copyright @ 2025 Susan E. Hartley

Copyright to the individual essays retained by the contributors.

All rights reserved. No part of this publication may be reproduced, stored in a retrieval system, or transmitted in any form or by any means- electronic, mechanical, audio recording, or otherwise- without the author's written permission.

www.globalvoices4peace.ca

Issued in print and electronic formats

ISBN 978-1-0691802-0-9 (pbk) – ISBN 978-1-0691802-1-6 (ebk)

Cover Illustration: Feodora Chioosea / Istock.com
Editor Photo by Amy MacConnell
Cover &Interior Design by C. Hartley
Back Cover Quote - Yamoussoukro Declaration on Peace in the Minds of Men (Yamoussoukro, Côte d'Ivoire, 1 July 1989).

First Edition Printed in Canada 2025

We are all different, and yet...

We want to be safe.

We want to eat good food.

We want our children to get a good education.

We want a safe place to call home.

We want to be able to see our family or chosen family.

We want to contribute.

We want to laugh.

We want to be loved.

We want to do what we love to do.

We want to be healthy.

We want to be respected.

We want to live in peace.

We are all different, and yet we are all the same.

~ Shannon O'Rourke-Kasali

To hope is to give yourself to the future - and that commitment to the future is what makes the present inhabitable.

- Rebecca Solnit, *Hope in the Dark: The Untold History of People Power*

Table of Contents

Preface

Peace cultures thrive on and are nourished by visions of how things might be, in a world where sharing and caring are part of the accepted lifeways for everyone.
- Elise Boulding

Global Voices for Peace started as a response to a feeling of tension that bordered on despair and helplessness. As someone who dedicates time and energy to advocating for human rights, justice, and equity I felt this sense of despair, reinforced with images of violence and destruction, all too often in the news and on social media newsfeeds.

I belong to a community of peacebuilders and social justice advocates who work tirelessly at their vocation and have been doing so for decades. Yet, we continue to see conflict throughout the world. Those who study the numbers and statistics of peace and conflict assert that, at this time in history, we are witnessing the highest levels of violence, war, genocide, and human migration our planet has ever seen.

This led me to ask some questions: We know who wages war, but do we know who is waging peace? We can name the great military generals and heroes of war, but do we recognize the peacebuilders among us? We are overwhelmed daily by war-related stories, images, and video clips, but where are the stories of peacebuilding? The story of war, battles, and conquest is taught as history to our children, but how is peace taught?

If you follow the media it seems that war and conflict are more worthy, somehow, of our attention. This just doesn't make sense.

The more I thought about it, the more I felt I wanted to find a way to promote the work that peacebuilders are doing. Ideas for what *Global Voices for Peace* would become began to germinate.

In my professional work, as a clinical psychologist, I have helped individuals and families make difficult and sometimes transformative changes in their lives. Early in my career I realized that, more often than not, the root of their distress was related to social inequity, violence, or discrimination. I began to advocate on their behalf and, more broadly, for social change. I began to work with not-for-profit organizations that were advocating for economic and social equity, and I developed and taught a graduate course in Clinical Psychology on Organizational and Systems Change.

In 2009, I took my interest in social justice and human rights beyond the local level and, through engagement with the organization Right to Learn Afghanistan (formerly Canadian Women for Women in Afghanistan), I worked to raise public awareness about the plight of women and girls in Afghanistan.

In early 2015 I was encouraged to apply for a fellowship in Peace and Conflict Studies at the Rotary Peace Centre at Chulalongkorn University in Bangkok. I was fortunate to be selected to study there in 2016, along with twenty other fellows from 16 different countries. It was then that I began to claim my identity as a peacebuilder and to understand that the social justice work I was involved with was, in essence, peace work.

Since that time, I have continued to work from a peacebuilding perspective locally and globally.

In 2016 I coordinated the Women's Peace Tables Worldwide along with my Peace Fellow colleague, Ellen Maynes, and in collaboration with Irene Santiago (#womenseriously) and Peace Women across the Globe.

In 2017 I had the immense privilege of returning to the Peace Centre in Bangkok to teach a new cohort of Peace Fellows on the topic of Gender, Peace, and Conflict.

My peace advocacy also includes promoting population health locally and nationally through policy development related to addressing economic, social and cultural inequities. My work is varied yet focused on helping non-governmental organizations that work to address human rights issues, poverty, and social justice issues.

All that to say, I have embraced my inner peacebuilder.

As I began to work more directly on peacebuilding projects around the world, I developed a better understanding of the work being done in different regions. I became a member of a network of dedicated individuals from different organizations across the globe. I was impressed by the passion and professionalism being brought to bear in the peacebuilding movement; actions that were going mostly unnoticed by the media and not present in the general consciousness.

The idea of gathering the thoughts and reflections of these incredible people and sharing them began to take shape. I started by asking those in my network to send me their one-page reflections on the following questions:

"What needs to happen for humanity to find a way to peace for our world, our communities, and our societies? What actions can we take now to move peace forward?"

The response was immediate and, in some ways, surprising. Clearly, I was not the only one who felt we needed to elevate the voices of those working in peace. The reflections that I received were truly thoughtful and inspiring. Respondents offered their encouragement for the project and commented on how important and timely they thought this project was - *it is what the world needs now*. Many offered to share the questions and the invitation to contribute, on my behalf, with their colleagues and networks. As a result, the contributors truly offer a worldwide perspective.

The contributors to *Global Voices for Peace* are a small, representative group of peacebuilders; there are so many more people working in peace than this book could possibly accommodate. I expect we will continue to hear more about what is happening in the field as we elevate these voices.

I believe every contributor to the anthology is an active peacebuilder. However, some of the contributors insisted that they do not see themselves as peacebuilders, even though, in many cases, they have devoted their life work to what I would describe as essential peacebuilding.

And so, what is my definition of a peacebuilder? I had the immense pleasure of meeting the Bangladesh Ambassador to the UN, Anwarul Chowdry, at the wrap-up of the 2016 Women's Peace Tables Worldwide in New York City. He was the key advocate for the adoption of a Culture of Peace approach in our world and so I turn to him when I consider the question: Who are the peacebuilders?

> *"I have seen time and again how people – even the humblest and the weakest – have contributed to building the culture of peace in their personal lives, in their families, in their communities and in their countries – all these contributing to global peace one way or the other."* ~ Ambassador Anwarul Chowdry[1]

---

[1] https://www.globalissues.org/news/2020/10/22/26958

As the contributions flowed in I noticed that certain themes began to emerge which led to the organization of the chapters in this book. They reflect the observation that peacebuilding happens at the individual, relationship, community, regional and global level and that every day there are opportunities for each of us to create peace.

A publisher once told me that any book with the word "Peace" in the title would not be successful. So how will I measure the success of *Global Voices for Peace*? I have three goals in mind that, if achieved, will make the anthology a success.

The anthology is an introduction to people around the world who are building peace, from frontline advocates to journalists, politicians, artists, academics, and everyday peacebuilders. It is an introduction to concepts, perspectives, and opinions as diverse as the contributors to this anthology - from over 50 different nations spanning the globe. If, after reading the book, you, the reader, come away with an increased understanding that peacebuilding is alive and well the world over, and that there is amazing work being done across the globe by dedicated individuals and organizations, and if the message of peace being possible stays with you, I have met my first goal.

If the contributors to the book and those working in the field of peacebuilding connect more, find further ways to support and collaborate, and continue to grow the peace network, then I will have realized my second goal.

Lastly, it is my dearest hope that the reader finds the contributions inspiring and will be motivated to look further into the contributors, their organizations and their projects.

Ultimately, I am hopeful that the reader will come to see that each of us can take conscious steps in our own lives to move toward making global peace a reality and become, in our own way, a peacebuilder.

From out of the community come the people and gifts necessary to initiate, support, help create and sustain the understandings that are reached.
John Paul Lederach, from *Reconcile: Conflict Transformation for Ordinary Christians*

Introduction

The pursuit of peace is an exhilarating adventure.[2]

---

[2] Yamoussoukro Declaration on Peace in the Minds of Men (Yamoussoukro, Côte d'Ivoire, 1 July 1989).

This book is an introduction to peacebuilders. Throughout the book certain themes emerge and, at times, repeat; themes supported by and grounded in years of academic studies on peace and conflict and the experiences of those practicing the work of peacebuilding. While peacebuilders share common roots in the history, development, and language of peace, and common goals in what we hope to achieve, the book illustrates that there are many diverse ways of contributing to the realization of those goals. This book offers a space in which these diverse voices can hold a conversation, witnessed by people around the world who are open and willing to listen to the hope they bring.

Since Plato's time, the search and striving for peace have been well documented. All of the world's religions have created guidelines or tenets for how to achieve peace, including, in some form, the principle of the 'golden rule', and philosophers throughout the ages have offered their thoughts on the possibility of peace and what it would mean.

As early as the seventeenth century educators were asserting that the way to achieve peace in the world was through education. Those early educators believed that understanding others and having shared values would overcome the differences that lead to conflict and provide a road to peace.

After the Napoleonic Wars in the nineteenth century, proponents of peace began to argue against the buildup of armaments and to study the threats of war. This peace movement was bolstered by the socialist political and workers' rights organizations of the time.

Between the two World Wars, the study of peace became more formalized and defined, with the issues of global peace and the accumulation of armaments more heightened as topics of peace research and discourse. After World War II, peace studies appeared as an academic discipline with the establishment in 1948 of the peace study program at Manchester College in the United States.

The formalization of peace as an area of research and study was subsequently bolstered by the establishment of the Peace Research Institute Oslo in 1959 and the first university-based School of Peace Studies in 1973 at Bradford University in England. Since then, peace study programs have been established throughout the world, and organizations and universities have supported peace studies through fellowships and funding.

While peace has been a topic of discussion throughout most of human history, there has been an evolution over time in what we mean by peace, how we research, study and learn about peace, and how we practice peace.

The language of peace starts with the word itself, and many of the contributors to this book raise the question: "What is Peace?" Indeed, how can we weigh in on how to bring peace to our world if we don't articulate how we will recognize the goal?

Is peace the absence of conflict? Or, rather than being defined by the absence of something, can we construct an entity that is peace as defined by structures, attitudes, and institutions that are present? Or is peace a process rather than a state? Or both? How does peacebuilding intersect with other disciplines, actions, campaigns, and approaches to building a healthier and more secure world?

How we understand and build peace at this time in history is highly influenced by the foundational contributions of Johan Gultang, John Paul Lederach, the United Nations, and the proponents of a Culture of Peace.

Johan Galtung is credited as being the principal founder of the discipline of peace and conflict studies, and for introducing the concept of peace into academic literature. Galtung distinguished between two types of peace: positive peace and negative peace.

Students, researchers, and practitioners act with a common, or collective, vision in which they work toward creating a world where "all people and the natural environment flourish, thrive and prosper," and where everyone can reach their full human potential, and live with social justice.[3] This vision is based on a commitment to equality in human rights, conflict transformation, peacebuilding,

---

[3]Mauro, A.V. The New Geneva. Arthur V. Mauro Centre for Peace and Justice, St. Paul's College, University of Manitoba (2003)

social justice, and truth and reconciliation.[4] This is what Gultang refers to as positive peace.

While negative peace is defined by what is not there - the absence of violence - positive peace is primarily defined by what is present. Frameworks such as the Pillars of Positive Peace (Institute of Economics and Peace), the United Nations Sustainable Development Goals, and the social and structural determinants of health as described by the World Health Organization are based on this concept: what needs to be in place to build peace and systems that are resilient in the face, or threat, of crisis or conflict. Research in positive peace and indicators of peaceful states identifies peace occurring when a community has non-violent ways to resolve differences, when human rights are present, and when social justice is the norm. As we identify the actions, attitudes, institutions and structures that support peace, we create a practice of peacebuilding that focuses on creating these conditions in our communities and our world.

In the 1980s John Paul Lederach introduced the concept of conflict transformation to peacebuilding with the view that to sustain peace we must transform conflict, rather than resolve or manage it, and that the goal of transformation is healthy local and global relationships and communities. His 1997 book *Building Peace* is considered to be a classic in the discipline of building peace.

In the 1990s the United Nations was challenged to lead global efforts to promote positive peace. In 1992 UN Secretary-General Boutros Boutros-Ghali released his report *An Agenda for Peace*. In this report, Boutros-Ghali introduces the concept of post-conflict peacebuilding, suggesting that it is insufficient to only consider peacemaking and peacekeeping when addressing the topic of peace.

Boutros-Ghali defines "post-conflict peace-building" as "action to identify and support structures which will tend to strengthen and solidify peace in order to avoid a relapse into conflict."[5]

---

[4] ibid

5 Boutros-Ghali, Boutros (1992). "An Agenda for Peace". International Relations. 11 (3): 201–218.

This was followed in 1999 by the adoption of *The Declaration and Programme of Action on a Culture of Peace.*[6] The goal of a Culture of Peace is to work toward a positive peace of justice, tolerance, and equity, and identify values, attitudes and behaviours that would reject violence, prevent conflict by addressing root causes, and solve disputes through dialogue and negotiation. The provision of peace education based on the principles of a Culture of Peace was identified as key to promoting positive and sustainable peace.

In September 2023, UN Secretary-General António Guterres launched a New Agenda for Peace, "presenting a vision for how the international community can more effectively prevent conflict and sustain peace at a moment when the world is experiencing unprecedented and overlapping crises."[7]

Peacebuilding, while a discreet discipline and area of study, overlaps with peacemaking and peacekeeping in definition and practice. Peacebuilding, peacemaking, and peacekeeping are necessarily connected, yet like a Venn diagram illustrating approaches to Peace and Conflict, they occupy unique space as well as interconnected and interdependent spaces.

Peacebuilding occurs through practices and policies that transform relationships and the fundamental social and systemic attitudes, institutions, and structures that support injustices and conflict. Peacemaking works to resolve conflicts after they erupt, most often through peace negotiations and dialogue. Peacekeeping seeks to stop or limit violence without addressing the causes and often plays a role in enforcing the agreement arrived at through the peacemaking processes.

In this book peacebuilders, peacemakers and peacekeepers share their views on how to build sustainable peace in our world. This community of peace practitioners is a multi-faceted, intersectional, and diverse group of people who understand that peace is not a stand-alone process but impacts - and is impacted by - all aspects of our human experience.

Enjoy the conversation and thanks for listening.

---

6 http://www.un-documents.net/a53r243a.htm

7 https://www.undp.org/blog/five-things-know-about-new-agenda-peace

Chapter One: Peace Is Possible

It isn't enough to talk about peace. One must believe in it. And it isn't enough to believe in it. One must work at it.
- Eleanor Roosevelt

Shortly after I completed the Rotary Peace and Conflict Studies program in 2016, I went to a meeting with another psychologist. He greeted me with a sarcasm-laden question: "Do you really believe in world peace?" The despondency, powerlessness, and hopelessness in his question were palatable and understandable. After all, peace is not at the forefront of our common and public discourse. It hides in the back pages of our media, if there at all. I am grateful to this man, as it confirmed for me that we need to talk openly and more frequently about the possibility of peace in our lives and in our world.

The first chapter of the book starts by inviting you to delve into the minds, hearts, and experiences of people working in peace in a way that helps us to understand how people can have hope in a world where so many people - too, too many people - experience the consequences of personal, systemic and structural violence and conflict.

From personal experiences of peace to the intensity and importance of sharing stories and building relationships based in peace, to recognizing our responsibility to each other and the natural world, these reflections offer ways forward for us all.

Curiosity, listening, living authentically and intentionally, connecting within and between, sharing stories, and committing to each other and the goal of peace - these are all gifts that these peacebuilders offer in this chapter.

I dream of a world in which we are not separated from each other by fear, suspicion, prejudice or hatred; in which we are free and equal, considerate and loving with each other.
- Adam Curle

Rukmini Iyer - India

Rukmini Iyer is an India-based peacebuilder, leadership consultant, and dialogue facilitator with over two decades of global experience. Integrating ecocentrism, conscious leadership, and conflict resolution, she bridges corporate leadership and grassroots peacebuilding to nurture sustainable, compassionate communities. She is also a writer, adjunct faculty, Rotary Peace Fellow, and Vital Voices Fellow.

A Field Beyond Right and Wrong

In the depths of our shared humanity lies an ancient truth: peace is not the opposite of war, but a capacity waiting to be reclaimed. It is not an event, nor a fleeting state, but a choice – a quiet power that transcends the binaries of victory and defeat, right and wrong.

To bring peace to our world, our communities, and our societies, we must first reclaim it within. This is not the peace of treaties and tabled negotiations, but the peace that rests in acknowledging our shared smallness, our vulnerabilities, and our infinite potential. It begins when we step away from the need to dominate and define power through conquest or accumulation. It takes root when we dare to find our power within and use it to nurture, to create, and to connect.

Imagine a world where power is no longer hoarded in institutions but shared through acts of care. Where people find dignity in the simple act of preparing a meal, growing food, or tending to one another's wounds.

Where ambition is not the relentless pursuit of more but the quiet courage to pursue joy, community, and fulfilment. This is not utopia; it is the reality of billions who live in peace even now – tending gardens, creating art, building homes, working through conflicts, falling in love, raising children, and sometimes, walking away from situations that can no longer be nourishing or resourceful.

The conditions for peace are already here, hidden in the smallness of everyday life. But peace cannot thrive in isolation. It demands that we engage with the "inner terrorists" within ourselves – the fears, prejudices, and ignorance that fuel exclusion and violence. It calls on us to recognise the humanity in those we marginalise, even those who threaten us. To see not only the victims of violence, but also the broken soul behind the gun, and to ask: what must we heal in you, so that you no longer seek your voice in destruction?

Action is the bridge between the peace within and the peace without. It is in the choices we make daily: to listen deeply, to speak responsibly, to see beyond borders, and to nurture spaces where every life – be it a refugee child, a farmer, or an artist – feels valued and seen. It is in reclaiming our words, resisting narratives that dehumanize, and choosing to call things by their true name – not Islamic States, or right-wing governments, or dictatorships, but fractured, fearful humans.

Out beyond the noise of wrongdoing and rightdoing, there is a field. If we dare to step into it together, we may find that peace is not something we achieve but something we become. And in that becoming, we transform not just ourselves, but the very world.

All of our humanity is dependent upon recognizing the humanity in others.

– Desmond Tutu

Sellah N. King'oro - Kenya

Dr. Sellah N. King'oro is a peace and security specialist and an advocate of the High Court of Kenya. In 2023 she received a presidential trailblazer award in women, peace and security from the Kenyan president. and a shortlisted award medal from the Women in Defence UK in the inspirational category. She is the Senior Gender Advisor at the British Peace Support Team (Africa) where she builds the capacity of Troop and Police Contributing Countries to deploy quality military and police personnel to UN/AU peace support operations in Africa. She has contributed to reconciliation/ dialogue processes among communities in parts of East, Central, and West Africa. Dr. King'oro is a post-doctoral fellow at the Institute for Genocide and Mass Atrocity Prevention (IGMAP), State University of New York, USA. She has a PhD in Peace and Conflict Studies and an MA in International Studies. She is a Rotary Peace Fellow.

I Am Because We Are

Peace is like a bird in the hands of a young boy who asks a wise man if the bird is dead or alive. If he says it is alive, the boy will crush the bird and kill it. If he says it is dead, the boy will release the bird.

Humanity has the power to stifle peace or to let it thrive. The push to strangle peace is driven by greed.

Collier & Hoeffler's greed and grievance theory (2004) [8] argues that greed causes conflicts due to the desire for more resources or power, while grievance arises from perceived injustices or inequalities. While democracy aspires to distribute power equitably in a society, people have found ways to manipulate democratic institutions to feed personal interests instead of addressing collective needs. To a great extent, rebellion in African democracies is motivated by the potential realization of economic gains.

Two main conditions that can enable the achievement of peace in the world are Ubuntu and servant leadership.

Nelson Mandela reminded us that Ubuntu is the profound sense that we are human only through the humanity of others.

---

[8] From "Greed and Grievance in Civil War", Paul Collier and Anke Hoeffler, Oxford Economic Papers, Vol.56, No. 4(Oct. 2004) pp. 563-595

It is the Ubuntu spirit that builds my definition of peace. If each person in the world believes that 'I am because we are', we shall NOT put our own interests above those of our compatriots. By doing so, greed is transformed into selflessness thereby making leadership a service to others, not an opportunity to gain power. In this way then, Rotary's motto of service above self is demonstrated in our lives.

There is hope for peace in the world. We have celebrated many selfless leaders like Martin Luther King Jr, Mother Teresa, Nelson Mandela, Kwame Nkrumah, and Prof. Wangari Maathai, among others.

The fact is, yes, we can do it! We can be the selfless generation that humanity needs to reinstall peace and conquer violence.

Barbara Walshe - Ireland

Barbara Walshe has worked in the fields of research, advocacy, training, community development, peacebuilding, and restorative work at local, national, and international levels. Her current work in restorative justice stems from a growing need among human beings, communities, and institutions to address and reflect on the effects of harm. She worked with former Supreme Court Justice Janine Geske, at Marquette University's Restorative Justice Dept. in Wisconsin, United States. Barbara has facilitated dialogue with survivors of institutional abuse in Ireland. She is a former President of the Board at the Glencree Centre for Peace and Reconciliation and is active and committed to peace and reconciliation on the island of Ireland by promoting dialogue between different traditions and faiths. She is currently working for the European Network for Remembrance and Solidarity in Warsaw, Poland. Barbara has an MA in Community Development, an MA in Reconciliation and Conflict Transformation, and is a Certified Mediator and Trainer.

I Believe in Small Things

A lifelong Jewish activist for peace in her late sixties stood on the Israeli side of Checkpoint 300 in Bethlehem, one of the many barriers Palestinians must navigate to get to work inside Israel every day. I stood on the Palestinian side of the barrier; my job was to help where I could and to monitor behaviour. When I asked Ofra why she stood here, she replied, 'I believe in doing small things.'

A strong advocate for the security of Israel, she was also concerned about the needs of Palestinians for their security so that they were able to go to work and feed their families. She also explained that while she could not change the political situation, she was determined that Palestinians would get at least an opportunity to engage with one Jewish person who wanted to help them, albeit in a small way. She was also concerned for the often young Israeli soldiers at the checkpoint, and engaged with them when she could, to raise their awareness of what they were doing to both the Palestinians and themselves by being there.

Although she had experienced devastating losses in her own family because of the Holocaust, she rejected hatred and violence and wanted to be a visible and positive example for change and peace.

We can say we have no power to change anything. We can say that we are afraid. We can each say that 'it is none of my business'. In the end, it is 'all of our business.' Small things are big things: rejecting the chorus of prejudice, "speaking the truth' instead of maintaining silence, taking an opportunity to 'talk to the enemy' - the perceived other that is different from us, as well as being curious and respectful of what people believe, rather than using our religion as a weapon to denigrate another's faith, and being willing to listen, really listen to hear rather than defend.

I believe in small things.

Carole St. Laurent is an award-winning blogger. Believing there is nothing more powerful than personal stories to nurture peace, she has taken her pen and camera around the world to capture these stories. She actively empowers youth as peacebuilders through the "Are We Together?" peace curriculum. Carole is a Rotary Peace Fellow and holds a Postgraduate Diploma in Peace and Conflict Resolution from Makerere University, Uganda.

www.crypeace.org

We Are One Global Family

I have a dream: that people recognize and live from the conviction that we are all members of the One Global Family. If we do, it will change the world.

It's true that all people are unique in our individuality, equal in our rights, and united in our shared humanity. We are One Global Family. However, today, we do not equally enjoy its privileges, and we mistake parts for the whole. Only by understanding at a deep, personal level that we are, indeed, members of One Global Family, and that our future as a species is united, whether for good or for ill, will we find the conviction, motivation and perseverance to pursue justice and generosity tenaciously, until all children everywhere can sleep in peace.

My love for the One Global Family, and my conviction that it is a foundational principle that can unite us in global goals versus divisive struggles, has drawn me to many countries around the world. I spent over three years in Africa, and another year visiting virtually every region of the world. By asking people what peace means to them, and whether they are experiencing it, I have learned about the burdens of conflict and poverty and witnessed heroism and resilience.

Insightful and inspiring responses have been shared by street youth and former abducted child soldiers in Uganda, Syrian refugees in Türkiye, Indigenous people in Panama, bikers in Canada, peacebuilders in the Occupied Palestinian Territories, Rwanda, and Cyprus, and ordinary people in Israel, El Salvador, Cambodia, the Democratic Republic of the Congo (DRC) and beyond.

I have learned that it is not the circumstances of our lives, nor the ability of our bodies, but the attitude of our souls that brings deep peace.

In the West, people primarily define peace as a personal pursuit. This is a luxury. In conflict zones, people define peace as political hope. In underdeveloped nations, people define peace as daily survival. But we all want peace. We all deserve peace.

Beyond sharing people's stories, I want to help shape people's future stories. That's why I founded CryPeace.org – to inspire people to live as members of the One Global Family and to empower youth as peacebuilders. We do so through a free peace curriculum, called "Are We Together?"

I have come to realize that love is the path to peace. Love for self inspires us to personal growth while being gentle on ourselves when we fall short. Love for others empowers us to treat others as we would have them treat us – a core teaching of all the world's major religions.

Love for the earth inspires us to care for it and use its resources wisely. Love for others compels us to share the earth's resources equitably. If you are ever unsure of how to seek peace, ask, "What would love do?" Love will direct your steps.

Let's commit to being the most loving versions of ourselves as possible, and to raising a generation for peace. These are the most powerful, possible, investments in peace that I can imagine.

Are we together?

When we see the world through each other's eyes, we'll learn how much we are brothers and sisters, siblings in the One Global Family.
- Carole St. Laurent

Marie Burge works for systemic change toward the elimination of poverty and the eradication of excessive concentration of wealth. She is a founder/member of Cooper Institute Collective (1984) and has about fifty years of experience working on issues of social justice—both in Prince Edward Island, Canada and in the Dominican Republic.

Restless Peace: On the Path to Peace

At the risk of jumping into the weeds of English grammatical parsing, I dare to claim that "peace" is not only a subject or object in a sentence. I want to break with the norm and think of "peace" as a predicate, a simple verb. Some of peace's sister words such as hope, belief, harmony, equality and even democracy have verb derivatives. My challenge to myself and to others is to think of peace not only as our goal or aspiration but as the dynamic action, the peace evolution.

In this frame of mind and heart, the concept of the peace "movement" has a significance. We are on our way. We are ever on a path to peace. Interior peace is found on that path. We are not "at peace", rather we are in the process of peace. Peace is the dynamo which leads us to move toward further and newer stages of peace evolution. Ours is a restless peace.

The pathway to peace is grounded in principles of human dignity and the dignity of all of nature. This dignity can be realized only when we recognize the collective rights of human persons and the rights of the planet and the universe (maybe even multiverses).

Wars and all aggression constitute a paralyzing roadblock on the path to peace. War is based on the violation of the most fundamental of rights, the very right to autonomous existence. The meaning of peace is diminished by "peace talks" which merely aim at the "ceasing of hostilities".

On the path to peace, we will engage with a suite of interrelated systemic violence: poverty, classism/casteism, racism, ageism, ableism, elitism, multiple gender discriminations, gender-based violence, and the warming of the planet.

Ela Bhatt speaking about poverty goes so far as to say that when we remain silent, we are giving "social consent to let the situation continue. For this reason, I say that our silence is violent. Looking the other way is a form of consent. It is our moral failure that we still tolerate poverty."

(Ela Bhatt, in the 2013 Gandhi Lecture on Nonviolence at McMaster University).

In our journey on the path to peace, we meet a multitude of violent and powerful obstacles created by systems created by profit-hungry humans. While we are railing against these - and we must do that - we need to be convinced that peace is a spiritual undertaking.

We are united and connected to restless hearts around the world who believe that we are together on the path to peace and are willing to be peace evolvers committed to action.

"Peace is not the product of a victory or a command. It has no finishing line, no final deadline, no fixed definition of achievement. Peace is a never-ending process, the work of many decisions."

– Oscar Arias (Former President of Costa Rica, 1940 – present, Costa Rica)

Martin Rutte is an international speaker and consultant. He is president of Livelihood, a management consulting firm with offices in New Mexico, USA and Prince Edward Island, Canada. The company's areas of service include: strategic vision, corporate spirit, performance management, facilitated dialogue, and bold leadership. He is a co-author of The New York Times Business Bestseller, *Chicken Soup for the Soul at Work*.

Sustainable, Permanent World Peace – A Call to Action

In a world where the mere mention of Sustainable, Permanent World Peace often elicits skepticism, disillusionment, and a sense of impossibility, it's easy to feel stuck in a narrative devoid of hope. But what if we dared to rewrite this story?

Picture this: you hold a magic wand in your hand. It's a doorway for manifesting your deepest desires. What if, with a wave of this wand, you can co-create a world where Sustainable, Permanent World Peace reigns? Not just an absence of conflict, but a tapestry woven with threads of harmony, respect, and boundless opportunity for all.

Go ahead, wave the wand right now. And remember, every journey, no matter how monumental, begins with a single step. It doesn't have to be grandiose; it just needs to be a promise to yourself, a commitment to take a small, tangible action within the next 24 hours, and then in the next 24 hours after that, and so on and so on.

By embracing this simple step, you're not merely dipping your toes into change; you're forging a path towards a brighter future. Any excuse you give yourself for inertia maintains the status quo, while every step forward initiates a seismic shift towards a new reality – one where peace isn't just an aspiration, but a tangible existence, a true Heaven on Earth.

This is a call to action, a rallying cry to unite in pursuit of a common vision and a shared destiny. Envision the boundless possibilities that await when Sustainable, Permanent World Peace becomes our collective reality – a world where security and respect are the cornerstones, and where humanity thrives in unity.

Are you in? Let's breathe life into the notion of Sustainable, Permanent World Peace, transforming it from a distant dream into a tangible, achieved reality.

Together, let's make it happen...beginning right now.

Stephanie Urchick - USA

Stephanie Urchick, a member of the Rotary Club of McMurray, PA, is the Rotary International President for 2024-2025. A Rotarian since 1991, Stephanie has participated in a variety of international service projects, including National Immunization Days in India and Nigeria, the building of an elementary school in Vietnam, water filter installation in the Dominican Republic, and mentoring new Rotarians in Ukraine. Her professional background is in the higher education, consulting, and entertainment industries. Stephanie received her doctorate in Leadership Studies from Indiana University of Pennsylvania. Rotary brings together 1.4 million people of action from all continents and cultures who partner with communities to find long-term solutions to the world's most persistent issues. Creating peaceful, welcoming, and inclusive societies is at the heart of what Rotary is all about.

Peace is Possible and it Starts within Each of Us

Peace.

A simple word describing a complex journey. How does our world achieve peace? Where does peace start? It has to happen before wars start, and before hostages, land and access to water, and religious rights are taken.

It has to start within us. Of course, that is easier said than done; but it is the only real and lasting way.

Peace is not a geographical line; it is a state of mind. We can learn peace, but it has to start within each of us.

The optimal condition for a peaceful society is one in which EVERY person views every other person as a family member - a member of the human race.

We know that this is not the current state. In fact, we aren't even close to it. But there are glimmers of hope in our societies.

Places exist where peace continues to be promoted: in our houses of worship, humanitarian organizations, service clubs, and in many other groups that understand how diversity, equity, and inclusion all lead to belonging.

We all belong to one big human family that shares this planet. We all deserve to see and feel peace.

Harriet Lamb - UK

Passionate about environmental and social issues, **Harriet Lamb** is a leader who, in the UK and globally, helped build the Fairtrade movement which enables producers in the developing world, including in conflict zones, to have a fair deal. She has always seen fairness in trade as one way to build the economic underpinnings of peace. She led International Alert, a leading peacebuilding organization based in the UK and working around the world from Tunisia to the Philippines. Acutely aware of how the climate crisis is a contributory factor of conflict, she has worked at Ashden and currently leads WRAP, the global environmental NGO working to end waste and promote a circular economy. Harriet has written two books including *From Anger to Action, Inside the Global Movements for Social Justice, Peace and a Sustainable Planet*, with Ben Jackson, and published by Rowman & Littlefield.

Thoughts for Peace

These are testing times for us all. Peace is on the geopolitical backfoot and so many of us are constantly shocked, saddened, torn apart, depressed by the constant flow of news about fighting and bloodshed in too many countries. That is why I welcome practical steps that we can take, such as these six ideas:

1) Give whatever you can to charities working in conflict zones, offering badly needed humanitarian relief to people on both sides.

2) Help tackle the climate crisis which is at the root of so much rising conflict. As communities and countries face pressures with drought, record temperatures, fires and flooding, so too is conflict ticking up. Climate changes in Syria, Sudan, South Sudan, Mali – have all contributed to the conflict. We can all play a part in reducing greenhouse gas emissions. We can decide not to fly for a holiday; to not buy new clothes for a year - and just enjoy preloved finds from charity shops; to not waste any food – because, unbelievably, 10% of all greenhouse gas emissions come from food waste. These are small actions we can all take to tackle the climate crisis and help enable the switch to circular living when we live within our planetary boundaries and repair, reuse, refurbish or recycle.

3) Buy goods from social enterprises supporting smallholders caught up in

war. For example, I love coffee from women farmers in the DRC and olive oil from Zaytoun in Palestine.

4) Reach out with loving kindness to people including those with whom you do not agree. That little WhatsApp message saying you are thinking of people can mean so much to those who are down. Some of my colleagues at work were reeling after a dramatic election result and were buoyed up by a wave of support from the team. Peacebuilding means walking in someone else's shoes – that is a muscle we all need to build.

5) Support refugees fleeing conflict who have arrived in your country. Maybe you can be part of a community sponsorship scheme enabling people to find safety in your country or lobby your government to accept more refugees or welcome a refugee into your home if you have a spare room. For example, we have a great Homes for Ukrainians scheme in the UK, and I have enjoyed two guests from Ukraine.

6) Keep talking about peacebuilding as an alternative to conflict. At International Alert, where I worked, we were part of a coalition to raise awareness about the need for peacebuilding, trying to persuade governments to put more funds into peace. So often money can be found for conflict, but peacebuilding is left starved for funds.

Unbelievably, peacebuilding is not even a word in most dictionaries. Yet we know it can work, as it did in Northern Ireland. We need that concerted effort by us all to stop fighting and find long-term peaceful solutions.

Robert Atkinson - USA

Robert Atkinson PhD, is the founding director of the One Planet Peace Forum and the award-winning author of *The Story of Our Time: From Duality to Interconnectedness to Oneness* and *A New Story of Wholeness: An Experiential Guide for Connecting the Human Family.* This essay is adapted from *The Way of Unity: Essential Principles and Preconditions for Peace* (2025).

www.robertatkinson.net

Peace Is Not Only Possible...

Peace on earth is a vision shared by all the world's spiritual traditions. To get to this promised time, we are going through periods of transformation leading us to unity and wholeness.

Humanity has its own developmental stages, just like all other life forms. In the transformations of our collective childhood and adolescence, as people focused more on differences, separation persisted and expansion, confusion, turmoil, and conflict prevailed on greater and greater levels.

This natural growth process is finally giving way to a consciousness of global integration. The next step in humanity's evolution is clear. Humanity's age of collective maturity is dawning. It is now time to recognize the oneness and wholeness of human relationships. This culminating leap of consciousness depends upon seeing all things as one, where there is no "other" left

to exclude from the circle of the human family – or from the web of life.

Lasting peace in today's complex, divided world can only be the result of a conscious evolutionary process that is all-inclusive and comprehensive, involving the entire human family, young and old, rich and poor.

Our challenge consists of building out the necessary infrastructure of families, communities, societies, nations, and global governance, all founded upon unitive principles that will help realize the preconditions for global harmony and unity. Upon these will rest the also needed personal and collective transformations of consciousness to bring about the complete unity of the human family.

We are entering a time when the equality of women and men will be fully realized when a balance between the extremes of wealth and poverty will be fully realized, when freedom from all forms of prejudice will be fully realized, when harmony between science and spirituality will be fully realized, and when the protection of nature as a divine trust will be fully realized.

These and many more preconditions will, realistically, need to be met in a long, arduous journey to true interdependence, wholeness, and world peace.

Our collective peacebuilding efforts will be greatly enhanced by acknowledging that there is an organic process of implementing the necessary unitive principles – principles intended to bring about unity – in all levels of society to ensure the unity-in-diversity of the human family and its lasting peace.

Over many more decades and centuries of extensive, inclusive, and worldwide initiatives on all levels to empower individuals and communities, to engage in social action on all levels, to build vibrant, thriving, communities of coherence, peace will be the natural outcome of this ever-expanding, all-inclusive process of humanity realizing its inherent oneness.

From this holistic, long-term perspective, peace is not only possible but also inevitable. As humanity continues its evolution toward maturity, world peace will be the fulfillment of its culminating stage of development, the fruit – and realized promise – of its collective destiny.

Kiran Singh Sirah - USA

Kiran Singh Sirah passionately believes in the power of human creativity and the notion of a truly global multicultural society. In 2017, he was one of seven people worldwide selected to receive the Champion of Peace award at Rotary International Day at the United Nations in Geneva and was recently nominated to receive a National Education Association Martin Luther King Jr. Human Rights and Social Justice award. His passion includes mentoring marginalized youth and partnering with peace activists, artists, poets and other underserved folks and supporting them to become the story of change they wish to see in the world.

Storytelling; A Gift of Hope

In my line of work, I am inundated with stories all day, every day, and I love it. I believe passionately in the power that storytelling has to bring peace, tolerance, and understanding to our world. At the same time, we have entered an era of conflict that is taking new forms and spreads in ways that outstrip the power of the international community to respond.

We've seen Ebola roil West Africa, conflict destabilize Ukraine and here in the US, domestic terrorism threatens the idea of living in a harmonious society.

As some of these factors harness the power of story to draw in young people to their dangerous ideologies, it is clear that we need new conceptual lenses and creative approaches for how we can collectively build peace, mutual respect, and understanding and prevent conflict from taking hold in our communities. We need

to not only reveal stories that matter but also in places that matter, too, such as many of the cultural arenas—museums, libraries, arts festivals—that present the stories of who we are, where we come from, and importantly, where we're going.

A story, just like a symphony or a painting or a sculpture, never stands alone. It exists within a context. Whatever story you hear or read, there are always other stories underneath it, or off to the side. For every account you read in a history book, there are many more that are in the margins, or not on the page at all.

Telling stories is not solely about a single place or a single tradition, but it is something that connects us with a capability much more profound. It plays a crucial role in binding and helping communities flourish, things that are

32

essential to helping us understand how we can improve and better our world.

We can never underestimate the power of using our own stories when we know that a world of peace comes from a state of empathy, a state of belonging, and shared notions of joy, happiness, and suffering, all of which are fundamentally part of our human condition. A world of peace can come from deconstructing the stories that are destructive, enabling us to transform stories into the constructive, even if at the moment of their telling it's hard to see that potential.

I'm always talking about "building a better world." I never mind when people roll their eyes a little bit. It's a lofty phrase, a lofty idea, and I know that to some people it sounds impossible or at the very least ambitious. Particularly over the last few years, as we've faced crisis after crisis, the prospect of building a better world sounds difficult. But I think it's important to remember that hope isn't necessarily a feeling; it's a practice. Storytelling, much like peacebuilding, is a broad and nebulous movement to which we can all contribute and benefit from. We don't have to strive to change everything (or end all wars) all at once; each of us can contribute a little each day to make our communities better places to live. If a story moves your heart, it's likely to move others' hearts too. It's a project we can chip away at.

Building a better world, a better future, is something that we can do together, one story at a time. A little every day.

Chapter Two: Close to Home

The collective is made of the individual,
and the individual is made of the collective...
each and every individual has a direct effect
on the collective consciousness.

Inner balance is crucial for peace work...
Engaged peace workers need to be strong,
stable, and genuinely peaceful.

Of course, you do not have to wait
until you achieve perfect peace and harmony
before you engage in social action.[9]

---

[9] From "*Creating True Peace: Ending Violene in Yourself, Your Family, Your Community*", Thich Nhat Hanh, Random House

In this chapter we are challenged to build practices of peace that are kind to ourselves, our families, our neighbours, and our communities, so that we may build a strong foundation from which we step outside of our comfort zones, live our ideals, and make a difference both close to home and in the world at large.

Practices of inner peacebuilding such as identifying those places and spaces that support calm, attending to personal well-being, and engaging in self-reflection, mindfulness, meditation, yoga, or other contemplative practices are all ways that peacebuilders lay that foundation.

Whether we are creating peace within ourselves, showing and teaching our children ways to peace, or being good neighbours, the reflections in this chapter capture the sentiment expressed by Rev. Michael Bernard Beckwith: *"Peace is in the journey, with every step we take. We carry it with us, and its impact is felt on a much wider scale. We all must find our own neighborhood, in our own community, where we're willing to share our gift. Many people don't realize that small groups of people around the world doing things with compassion have an impact on the mental and emotional atmosphere of the entire world."*[10]

In recognizing that our beliefs, emotions, and attitudes can direct our actions toward peace or conflict, these peacebuilders challenge us to engage in peace rather than conflict. Elise Boulding taught us that every day we encounter people who are different than us in some way and this provides an opportunity in which we must make a choice: whether to engage in that relationship with a view to peace or to conflict. Similarly, my work in conflict transformation has focused on how we transform relationships defined by difference or conflict into relationships of understanding and hope – through curiosity, inquiry and story sharing – even if we continue to disagree. It is not about sharing spoils or building walls; it is about creating space for difference through listening, sitting with it, and responding rather than reacting.

---

[10] From "Is World Peace Possible?" in Atkinson, R., Johnson, K. and Moldow, D. (eds.) (2020) *Our Moment of Choice: Evolutionary Visions and Hope for the Future.* New York: Atria Books

The power of education is captured in many of these reflections noting that education starts at the beginning of life, carries on through childhood, and into adulthood. Contributors speak of peace education that encompasses the practices of compassion, listening, and acceptance of the rights of the human and natural world. Elise Boulding stresses the importance of creating a peaceful worldview in children through providing opportunities in all settings and exposure to society outside of the home and school. Confucius is credited to have offered this wisdom: "*Education breeds confidence. Confidence breeds hope. Hope breeds peace.*" Mahatma Gandhi viewed children as our hope for real peace: "*If we are to teach real peace in this world, and if we are to carry on a real war against war, we shall have to begin with the children.*"

Our capacity for hope and openness, empathy and compassion, is affected by our own personal experiences of trauma. As you will read throughout this book, peacebuilding must consider the impact of trauma, not only on those directly affected by violence and conflict but also on those who do the work of peacebuilding.

Building peace begins close to home – with each of us.

Above all we must realize that each of us makes a difference with our life. Each of us impacts the world around us every single day. We have a choice to use the gift of our life to make the world a better place - or not to bother.
- Jane Goodall

Jill MacCormack - Canada

Jill MacCormack (she/her) is a neurodivergent writer/artist who lives with her family as a settler on Prince Edward Island/Epekwitk which is part of Mi'kma'ki, the traditional unceded territory of the Mi'kmaq people. A lifelong devotee of peace, Jill is also a nature lover, mindfulness meditation practitioner, gardener, environmental and social justice advocate and a devoted tea drinker who stumbles upon joy in unexpected places.

Expanding Our Caring: A Pathway to Peace

World Peace is something I wished for on every childhood birthday candle I blew out. Now I am older with a deeper understanding of my personal role in ending violence and creating Peace.

Peace is only possible by first learning to be with our own human hearts. Once we have found our Peace, we can then radiate this out to heal the greater world.

I use mindfulness meditation and self-compassion practices to reacquaint myself with the bright, loving and calm space within when the spinning world threatens to pull me from my center.

This training has fundamentally changed how I see and interact with thoughts, emotions and feelings about the circumstances of my life, which means it also changes the world around me. I cannot control how life might unfold but I can practice non-judgmental, present-moment awareness so that kind of responsiveness becomes my default instead of emotional reactivity.

Change is a constant in this world. Stillness is an option for quieting our minds so we can explore possibilities that widen our collective heartspace. Widen it such that no one and nothing is outside our range for compassionate responses, ourselves included.

A kinder, more compassionate world which takes reconciliation seriously, which centres those on the margins, which values all of life in its beautifully interwoven complexity and ensures that everyone's basic needs are met with dignity, is a world where greater Peace can take hold. This is how we heal intergenerational trauma. This is how we expand our caring. With time, we remember that we belong to each other and to Earth.

I welcome you to honour this present moment and the possibility it contains for choosing to be more Peaceful and compassionate people by recognizing the common humanity of our living breath; a pathway to Peace for all.

Tim Goddard - Epekwitk, Canada

Tim Goddard holds a PhD in educational administration and has 50 years of experience as an educator. His career has taken him from remote Pacific Island villages to First Nation, Métis and Inuit communities in northern Canada, from the Sámi towns of northern Sweden to Roma villages in the Balkans, from inner city Calgary to the industrial coast of Cape Breton, and in a variety of post-conflict environments in Afghanistan, Kosovo, and Lebanon.

Living in Harmony with People and Nature

I've never really thought of myself as a peacebuilder. As a teacher, my function is to try and get the most out of my students, to help them develop to their full potential. That requires them to understand the world in which they live so that they can continue to improve their personal circumstances and the circumstances of those around them – their families, friends, neighbours, and communities.

At this quarter mark of the twenty-first century, it is easy to despair of the future(s) we face. It is all too easy to observe our multiple challenges and be overwhelmed by a world in turmoil. We are beset by catastrophes both ancient and emergent. What can we, as a collective community, do to bring peace to the world, or at least our little corner of it?

In ancient days it was recognized that our world is an intricate web of interconnectivity. Scholars have determined that the 10 plagues of Egypt were all inter-related and followed each other in a specific order precisely because of these relationships. It was known that plague and pestilence were cohabitors of catastrophe, and so we only have four horsemen of the apocalypse – war, famine, plague/pestilence, death.

Over the past two or three millennia, we gradually ignored that knowledge. Now, in the 2020s, we recognize once more that environmental and population matters are interrelated, and that the only thing worse than death is disconnection.

Our contemporary horsemen are war, famine, environment/population, and disconnection.

There are those who suggest, only half in jest, that we should blow up the bridge, sink the ferry, and close the airport. "It worked during the pandemic", they say, and they may be right. I think that a more measured approach is warranted.

In most of the major religions, there is a rule about looking after your neighbours. This makes common sense. If I look after the neighbours on each side of my house, and they do the same, then two people will be looking after me. The community will be stronger if we all took care of those people who live on each side – not a huge imposition, surely?

We are fortunate on Prince Edward Island to have a strong tradition of caring for the land, but that stewardship is not automatic. There are those in our society, in all societies, who put self-interest before collective good. Collectively we need to protect the environment in which we and all other creatures live.

We live on an Island where people have lived for millennia: Epekwitk (Prince Edward Island) is located in Mi'kma'ki, the ancestral and unceded territory of the Mi'kmaq People.

It seems to me that a good start to peacebuilding here on Epekwitk would be to look to the lessons of the people who successfully stewarded this land for so long.

If we could each try to live a good, balanced life, which means respecting and protecting the environment and living in harmony with the people and creatures that live on the earth, and at the same time care for the neighbours on each side of us, then we can overcome those catastrophes, both ancient and emergent, with which we are and will continue to be faced.

Udaya Shanmugam - Sri Lanka/Canada

Udaya Shanmugam is a proud Tamil woman from Sri Lanka. She is a storyteller and a peace activist. She is dedicated to decolonizing and reclaiming the Indigenous practice of Yoga. As the founder of Yoga for Peace, she delivers free yoga programs for families affected by conflict. She is a Rotary Peace Fellow and completed a master's degree in Peace and Conflict Resolution at the University of Queensland. She holds a master's degree in Criminology and Law from the University of Toronto and is a certified mediator and negotiator working with human rights organizations in Kenya, Palestine, Pakistan, Sri Lanka and Greece (Lesvos). She is the co-founder of Culture Collective, an initiative led by Indigenous women to revive and preserve Indigenous cultures and facilitate global intercultural collaborations.

Embodying Peace:
An Invitation for Self-Discovery, Attending to Anger and Healing

From 1983 onwards Sri Lanka was embroiled in a bloody civil war. The island nation that was once dubbed as the jewel of the Indian Ocean and as God's own kingdom was in crisis. It still is.

Nadarajah Raviraj was many things - a husband, a father, a Tamil human rights lawyer, mayor of Jaffna, a Parliamentarian, a staunch supporter of Tamil sovereignty and a member of the Civil Monitoring Committee which monitored extrajudicial killings, abductions and disappearances in Sri Lanka.

On the morning of November 10, 2006, Raviraj engaged in a live studio interview, then had breakfast at his home, and shortly after, he drove out to his office, with his bodyguard. En route and just after 8:30 am, Raviraj was assassinated by a gunman on a motorbike on the streets of Colombo, the nation's capital.

Uncle Raviraj was shot five times. He was 44. We had lost our kin. I was 17 and even to this day I can recall with precise clarity the exact words and the tremble in my mother's voice as she informed me of his death.

It is widely believed that the government of Sri Lanka bears responsibility for the murder of Raviraj.

On that day, the world lost one of the most courageous defenders of human rights and peace. One can never fully recover from such a loss. The anger stemming from his death and the injustice of his assassination will always rage in my heart.

It is perhaps this very rage that makes me want to believe that peace is possible.

What if I told you that your breath is the most significant instrument you have at your disposal - a sacred tool which you can use at your will to ignite social change and create peace? Will you take my word for it?

The ancient Yogis and Yoginis believed that within each of us we hold all the power required to create the realities we desire for ourselves and our communities. The first step to creating our desired reality is dependent upon each one of us making a choice to raise our awareness and consciousness. How? By connecting with our breath we can discover how to realize peace.

So, why is it that more people don't venture towards this promised path of peace?

Often, this kind of inward journey of self-discovery in search of unshakable peace takes a certain level of curiosity, trust and courage.

Perhaps one of the greatest obstacles to connecting with our breath is the wounds and hurts we hold onto and find the most difficult to make peace with - a broken heart, a judgmental family, premature deaths, the betrayal of a lover or a friend, self-betrayal, family secrets, censored histories, collective trauma, violence, racism, injustice, genocide, colonization, discrimination. Human experiences and emotions that leave us vulnerable, naked and void.

A lack of true empathy and relatedness to comprehend the magnitude of loss and grief resulting from these human experiences only perpetuates our collective suffering. It inhibits us from ever achieving our desired realities for peace. Equally dangerous is one's inability to be honest with oneself about their wounds - their trauma.

It is difficult but it is not impossible to connect with the wisdom of our breath when we are still making our way through life's many currents and storms that cause deep pain, hurt and loss.

Peace is an inside project. Peace work starts within us. The deeper and the more sincere our commitment to heal from our many wounds, the higher the likelihood that we can begin the process of understanding the true power of peace. It is a process of internal self-discovery, excavation and inquiry.

With each inhale and exhale, take notice of your breath. You are the medicine. Peace begins with you.

Kimberly Weichel - USA

Kimberly Weichel is a Rotary Peace Fellow, author, educator, and non-profit leader who has worked at the forefront of building bridges between cultures and peoples for over 30 years. Her work has taken her to South Africa, East Africa, Southeast Asia, United Arab Emirates, Russia, Germany, Canada, and Australia as well as the U.S, where she has worked with consulting firms, non-profit organizations, international institutions including the United Nations, and others. Kim teaches at the Lifelong Learning Institute at American University in Washington DC, mentors young women, and advises non-profits. She is the author of several books, most recently *"Beyond Borders: One Woman's Journey of Courage, Passion and Inspiration (2016), Our Voices Matter: Wisdom, Hope and Action for Our Time (2019)* and *Uncovering New Possibilities: Insights From Our Time (2021).*
www.kimweichel.org

Pathways to Peace

As a lifelong peacebuilder, I find that the word *peace* is misunderstood. We often think of peace as an absence of conflict, but peace is a process and means so much more – it means dignity, well-being, and a nurturing environment in which each person can thrive and live a quality life.

As I write in my poem Pathways to Peace, "*Peace is a state of mind, a way of being. It is also a path of daily action. Peace is deep connection with myself and others, Peace is personal, political, spiritual and practical.*"

I prefer the word *peacebuilding* which refers to a committed process to actively build peace by all stakeholders. Peacebuilding encompasses many components to build a healthy environment - good governance, rule of law, a sound and inclusive educational system, a vibrant health care system, gender and economic equality, the ability to access jobs, affordable housing, and so much more.

So how can we live in peace? What actions can we take to build a peaceful society? My poem shares how we begin this journey – "*Peace starts with each one of us, Practicing, love and respect in our families, being good role models for our children, listening and speaking with love. Living peace means respecting differences, whether it be religion, culture, ethnicity or perspective, acknowledging that we each bring different gifts, knowing that we are interdependent.*"

Living in peace consciously requires many skills and commitment. One of my hopes is that every school will offer a required life skills course in which students learn basic communication, conflict resolution and emotional and social learning skills to enable them to develop healthy relationships. Another hope is core to my spiritual beliefs – that we strive to see each other as allies rather than competitors.

In each community and society, we must focus on overcoming the structural obstacles to peace: poverty, racism, sexism, and other forms of discrimination, economic inequality, and homelessness. Eradicating poverty, a UN Sustainable Development Goal, will ensure each person has food and shelter. Overcoming poverty is a fundamental human right and key to living in dignity. Combating racism and sexism and reducing structural inequalities, expanding the number of available jobs so that each person can access a decent job, and increasing affordable housing options so everyone has access to a decent home will all contribute to building a more peaceful society.

Every day, we have much work to do to build healthier and sustainable communities in which people can live more peacefully.

Peace is a pro-active and dynamic process: "*Peace means speaking up when we see injustice, taking a stand when we feel something is wrong, speaking our truth with others and being the change we wish to see.*"

My poem concludes: "*Peace starts with each one of us living it each day, with love and acceptance in our heart, and understanding as the common bond, that binds each of us on our various pathways to peace.*"

Cyrel San Gabriel - USA

Cyrel San Gabriel is the CEO of Editing Pro LLC, a US-based consulting firm providing editing and research services for international development agencies. She has worked in international development since 2006. In 2004 she started a Philippine-based consulting firm catering to donor-financed and government-funded projects. She is a Rotary Peace Fellow and holds a PhD in international conflict management from Kennesaw State University, Georgia, USA, and a master's degree in development communication and a bachelor's degree in broadcast communication, both from the University of the Philippines.

World Peace Begins with Me

Our world today is truly a mess—from war in Ukraine, Gaza, and Sudan to illegal migrants crossing the borders, refugees, drug smuggling, child trafficking, natural disasters, climate change impacts, widespread communicable and noncommunicable diseases, people living in inhumane conditions, rising inflation rates, corruption and injustice, high crime rates, discrimination (racial, religious, cultural, gender, age, economic)—and the list goes on and on. International agencies, governments, nonprofit organizations, the private sector, and highly influential groups and individuals are all making strides to help resolve these problems or at least alleviate the suffering of the affected innocent people, mostly women, children, people with disabilities, the elderly, and low-income groups.

As an ordinary citizen, what is my stake in these issues? Should I just relax and watch that heartbreaking news from the comfort of my home, feel bad in the moment, shrug it off, and move on with my life?

"World peace begins with me" may be a cliché but it is something that we need to remind ourselves constantly. I believe what we need is for everyone to do their part in whatever capacity they have.

At home, I can save energy and water. I can reuse and recycle materials such as jars, plastic bottles, papers, and old clothes. I can buy used wooden furniture and opt for paperless bills to help save trees. I can try not to buy clothes too often as garment manufacturing can harm wildlife and pollute soil and water.

When possible, I can walk instead of drive. In social media, I can spread words of hope and peace. I can buy goods from small businesses and from street vendors. If there are beggars on the streets, I can give them something useful (cold bottled water, freshly cooked food, or a few dollars). I can give to charitable causes.

As a business owner, I can create jobs and provide opportunities for those who are in disadvantaged situations. When people undermine me because of my race, I can choose to ignore it and go on with the business of becoming a better version of myself so I can help others do the same. Instead of whining and complaining, I can offer solutions (there's an exemption however, that is, when businesses provide a substandard service or a bad quality product, I can complain so they can make improvements).

There is no way of telling whether those things would have an impact on the world's problems at hand. I'm not trying to convince you to copy my lifestyle, but if everyone would step out of their comfort zone and give a helping hand, we will, in effect, spread peace in the hearts of those who feel hopeless. We can give them a ray of hope that they don't have to struggle alone, and we can give them that push to rise and become peacebuilders themselves.

World peace indeed begins with me.

Rosaline Obah - Cameroon

Rosaline Obah is a peace and community development specialist, and a national and international consultant in strategic communication, corporate crisis management, peacebuilding, public relations, and gender rights. She holds an international master's degree in Public Relations/Corporate Communications with a specialization in corporate crisis management. Among other positions she serves as the Cameroon Chapter President of the Young African Women Congress Network, the Vice National Coordinator of the Gender Data Network Cameroon and is an Ambassador of Global Peace Let's Talk. She is a Rotary Peace Fellow.

Bridging Divides: A Journey Towards Inclusivity and Peace

In a world marked by division, conflict, and polarization, there exists an urgent imperative to bridge divides and foster inclusivity. Our societies are grappling with myriad challenges that threaten to tear us apart. Yet, amidst the discord, there exists a glimmer of hope—a shared desire for unity, understanding, and peace.

Despite our diversity, we are all interconnected, bound together by our common aspirations for dignity, justice, and belonging. By embracing this shared humanity and reaching across divides with empathy and compassion, we can begin to dismantle the barriers that separate us and forge bonds of solidarity in our quest for peace.

Bridging divides requires a commitment to addressing the root causes of division, whether they stem from historical injustices, socio-economic disparities, or cultural misunderstandings.

It entails acknowledging the harms and legacies of colonialism, racism, and discrimination and confronting these injustices with humility and courage.

Three powerful tools for bridging divides and building peace are dialogue, education and technology.

Dialogue - open, honest, and respectful communication - seeks to understand rather than condemn, to listen rather than judge. Dialogue creates spaces for people to share their stories, express their concerns, and find common ground, even in the midst of disagreement. Through dialogue, we can challenge stereotypes, debunk myths, and humanize those whom we perceive as "other", fostering empathy and understanding across divides. Dialogue serves as a catalyst for reconciliation, healing, and transformation in our civil, political, and religious spaces.

Education promotes critical thinking, empathy, and intercultural understanding among future generations. By integrating diverse perspectives and histories into school curricula, we can counter stereotypes, challenge prejudices, and cultivate a culture of respect for diversity within our youth. Education empowers individuals to become agents of change in their communities, advocating for inclusivity, justice, and peace, and it lays the foundation for a more harmonious and interconnected world.

Fostering inclusive spaces creates opportunities for diverse voices to be heard and valued through meaningful participation and representation in decision-making processes. By amplifying marginalized voices and perspectives, we can challenge dominant narratives and promote a more pluralistic public discourse. Inclusive spaces provide platforms for building coalitions and alliances across divides, uniting individuals and communities in a common cause for peace and justice.

The responsible and ethical use of technology can be a powerful tool for bridging divides and fostering inclusivity. Social media platforms have the ability to connect people across geographic, cultural, and ideological boundaries, facilitating dialogue, collaboration, and solidarity. However, the proliferation of misinformation, echo chambers, and online harassment also poses challenges to building inclusive digital spaces. By promoting digital literacy, combating online hate speech, and harnessing technology for positive social change, we can harness the potential of technology to bridge divides and promote peace.

By embracing our shared humanity, engaging in dialogue, addressing root causes of division, and fostering inclusive spaces, we can build bridges that unite rather than divide us. In doing so, we can create a world where diversity is celebrated, differences are respected, and peace is not just a distant dream but a lived reality.

Diana Bonar is the Director and founder of Peaceflow and a partner of the U.S. Diplomatic Sector for gender equity through the Global Sports Mentoring Program Network. She is a Nonviolent Communication (NVC) facilitator with extensive experience in institutional development and conflict management. For a decade, she worked in communities affected by crime and violence alongside international peacebuilding Organizations. She is a Rotary Peace Fellow. www.peaceflow.com.br

Profound Change through Nonviolent Communication

Before every action, there is a belief. Beliefs generate thoughts, thoughts produce feelings, and feelings drive actions.

Throughout human history, we have witnessed violence, war, and genocide, and we continue to repeat these cycles. This suggests that we have not developed enough in changing the way we believe conflicts should be managed.

Before considering what we can do, we must examine what in our thinking contributes to our behaviors. I encourage you, as a reader, to reflect on the microcosm of your own life.

When you think about a distant war, you might feel powerless. My invitation to you is to reflect on how you use power. How do you engage with people who have different viewpoints? How do you raise your children? How do you lead your team?

Having worked with Nonviolent Communication (NVC), peacebuilding, and violence prevention for 15 years, I have learned several key lessons:

Anger management can save lives.

Emotional intelligence significantly impacts how people perceive reality and behave. This topic, along with NVC, should be taught in schools.

Empathy is a skill that people can learn to cultivate.

While some training aims to dehumanize others, NVC works to do the opposite.

Conflict indicates that something needs to change, not that we must annihilate the other party.

People can develop a new belief system based on power *with* others, not *over* them.

I firmly believe that integrating NVC into your personal life, work, and social interactions can bring about profound change.

Jenn Weidman is a facilitation, training, resilience, and peacebuilding professional working on peace and capacity building programs in Southeast Asia and globally. She is the founder of Space Bangkok, a social enterprise that helps those addressing conflict to do their best work by incorporating reflective and resilience elements in leadership development, facilitation, peacebuilding, capacity building, and other work.

Charlie Allen is a facilitation, resilience, leadership, and peacebuilding professional. His early experience is grounded in the security sector and over the past decade he has expanded his experience, working in South East, Eastern and South Asia, Western and Eastern Africa, MENA region and Oceania. He offers process facilitation, training design and delivery, resilience practice, leadership development, and organizational and community systems change.

Taking Care of Peacebuilders

The journey towards peace is long and challenging requiring deep reserves of hope and resilience.

So how do we care for the carers, heal the healers, and encourage the peacebuilders?

Too often we make strides in our work only to lose the very individuals who were seminal in our progress to burnout, depression, and worse. In the end, our systems and how we go about the work of peace are yielding a net negative.

We need to stop harming part of humanity in the process of trying to help another part of humanity.

Peace needs hope. And hope needs creative energy fueled by resilience. It needs all of us to be actively and intentionally stoking our inner sparks of energy through lifelong practice.

Our journey towards peace requires a fundamental shift in how we go about our work. It requires us to prioritize people and their wellbeing, to accept that resting and recharging are absolutely essential and should happen before we burnout and that the best and most crucial thing we can do as we work for peace is to first take care of our own wellbeing and resilience.

Investing in resilience must be seen not as indulgences, but as absolutely essential.

Eva Czermak - Austria

Eva Czermak is a medical doctor, mediator and Rotary Peace Fellow. For many years she worked as manager of an NGO providing medical help to marginalized people in Austria, helping refugees, poverty migrants, homeless people and drug-addicted people. In 2022 she changed her career. She now works in humanitarian aid in Ukraine for Caritas Austria, is involved in a health project in Burundi and other ongoing peace/dialogue projects. Eva is also a coordinator of the Rotary Peace Fellow Alumni Organization in Europe.

Learning and Practicing Peace

"Who will be the first one of you two to STOP?" is a question I like to ask my kids when they are fighting. Or sometimes it is preceded by physical separation, and I say, "I am now going to walk between you!" or "Go for a walk and come back only after you have cooled down!"

These are actually micro-versions of a ceasefire and starting peace negotiations. It is sometimes difficult to pull it off, but it can work.

I deeply believe kids are able to learn to manage conflict in this way and that they should be given the opportunity to do so! This is, for me, the most important starting point on the way to peace in our world. Teach our children healthy ways to communicate and collaborate. Teach it in school, teach it every day, and in a way that includes all children, so that no one is missed.

Positive ways to manage differences and conflict can be ingrained "into their DNA" in a positive way (the same way trauma can be ingrained - through repetition) and handed on to the next generation. The skills taught would include non-violent communication, conflict resolution, productive collaboration, positive imagining of one's own future, and the like.

A lot is happening already.

For example, there are "peace schools" in India, which take 30 minutes each morning to teach school-aged children and youth, peace related skills. A fellow peacebuilder runs a peace school in Congo, another one holds online courses connecting young people, teaching about war and its impacts, disarmament etc., and others teach mindfulness and meditation, or tension release and emotional control through sports. I've held workshops in schools teaching about reconciliation and discussing with pupils their own wishes how to best resolve conflicts.

A lot is possible and imaginable! We need more of it, in a more systematic way and more tightly knit.

Therefore, I think we should lobby for peace education to be integrated into the school curricula, for all school kids, worldwide. And in the meantime, we can start to experiment and develop culturally appropriate training materials and start to teach kids, where it is feasible, even outside the regular curriculum.

Martin Scott is a social entrepreneur, landscape architect, and peacebuilder who supports communities to foster positive peace through dialogue and conflict transformation. He is the Global Partnerships Manager of Mediators Beyond Borders International (MBBI) and a Rotary Peace Fellow.

StoryListening: A Key to Peace

In a world of endless information and countless tools for communication, the most valuable peacebuilding resource we possess is both free and nearly inexhaustible.

Major corporations have entire departments dedicated to communication and yet, not a single Director of Listening. We celebrate our storyteller-authors, movie directors, and musicians, but we lack a single award ceremony dedicated to the art of storylistening.

We all have experienced the dangers of what happens when we stop listening: ranging from angry voices and fractured relationships to extreme acts of violence. I remember watching the horrific events of September 11th and thinking, "This is how loudly someone had to speak to feel listened to."

Two things we know about someone who raises their voice: they care, and they don't feel listened to. If you ever catch yourself yelling, you similarly know it's because you care and you don't feel listened to. This is why someone simply repeating back to you what you said in a nonjudgmental way helps you to feel calmer. When you are yelling, one of the people not listening to you... is you.

Dr. Ken Cloke, founder of MBBI, outlines what occurs when we still don't feel listened to after raising our voices. The next stage is a demonstration of aggression, so our physical bodies reinforce our words, followed by violence towards others in a hope of garnering their attention, and finally, we resort to violence towards ourselves. Sadly, this escalation tracks globally as more people die from suicide annually than war, terrorism and natural disaster combined. When other forms of self-harm are included, we are 80 times more likely to kill ourselves than die at the hands of another human.

The positive news is the antidote for the deadliest form of violence facing our society is free. Committing to learning to be a better listener is free and there are almost an unlimited number of opportunities to practice. Thanks for listening.

Julie Pellissier-Lush - Epekwitk, Mi'kma'ki

Julie Pellissier-Lush is a Mi'kmaw storyteller, photographer, actor, drummer, best-selling author, and the first Indigenous Poet Laureate for Prince Edward Island (Epekwitk). Through her books, songs, poetry and other creative pursuits, Julie celebrates and shares the powerful stories of the Mi'kmaq on PEI. Julie is a cultural teacher and knowledge keeper. She finds inspiration from her elders as they bravely share their stories, and from today's courageous youth who are embracing and celebrating their rich culture. She is the recipient of the Queens Jubilee, Meritorious Service, and the Senators 150 Medals.

Let There be Peace on Earth and Let it Begin with Me

Sometimes late at night, this thought comes to me, what does peace mean?

Could peace be that we have no more war, everyone has enough food and land to be satisfied? Would that truly be peace? Even though this is really not a simple solution, once it is achieved would that be what peace is?

When I think of the state of the world I worry for this generation and the next and the next. Right now, in my home, I have someone I love deeply who is suffering from addictions.

What that means for me is there is no peace in my house. With the worry, the fighting, the days and weeks without a word, there is no peace in my heart and mind.

This is a smaller war many of us are struggling with, a fight everyday to find a safe place for them to heal, and there is nothing out there for them.

It has been a long time since I have had peace, in a much smaller context than world peace, but sometimes, as an old song I remember says, sometimes peace begins with the individual. That allows us to look farther than our own door to do the hard work to help bring peace to the world.

So individually it seems impossible to fix a broken world, but we can look after our friends and family, be there when needed and hope that healing works its way into a family, into the community, into the province, into the country, and slowly into the whole world.

Let there be peace on earth and let it begin with me.

Hilary Caldis - USA

Hilary Caldis is a women's empowerment activator working for the US Department of State. Prior to becoming a diplomat, Hilary founded and directed The Female Voice, a women's empowerment social media startup and creative agency. Hilary continues to propel women's rights and empowerment through her work as a diplomat, writer, designer, and entrepreneur. Hilary is a Rotary Peace Fellow.

Life-Centric Peacebuilding

The best advice I've taken, in peacebuilding and life, is taking the time to explore and prioritize my joys, talents, and desires as a pathway to doing sustained and impactful work.

I say this as burnout—exhaustion and feelings of negativism or cynicism related to one's job—is a major sticking point in peacebuilding work. Trying to transform the ugliest parts of society does, indeed, feel like thankless work when you don't like the work you're doing, or feel like it's not supporting your broader life goals.

I know it's pretty obvious advice, but it's amazing what we become willing to do when we get fired up over a cause.

In the short-run, it can be essential and growth-promoting to do things that we don't love, so long as we know there is an expiration date, like a shy person making some cold calls to support a political candidate. But for long-term work, we need to discern what we choose to do for our happiness and the causes we work to propel.

Sustained success as a peacebuilder is about finding the things that make us truly happy and making lifestyle-centric choices that harmonize who we are, what we're good at, what we want, and who we love. By doing this, we show up in life with all the different parts of ourselves in alignment rather than in parts.

As whole people, we naturally exude the happiness and peace required to make all the difference, be it running a UN humanitarian mission or calling up an old friend.

Lorelei Parker - Canada

Lorelei Parker, known by her ancestral name as Blue Thunder Spirit Woman, is the Team Lead for the city of Calgary's Indigenous Relations Office and is working to advance The City of Calgary's commitments to Truth and Reconciliation. Lorelei is also a consultant with Mediators Beyond Borders International and Canadian Equity Consulting, cultivating projects that focus on Indigenous relations, anti-racism and enhanced diversity, equity, inclusion and belonging efforts. @everydaypeacebuilder

Everyone, Everywhere, Everyday

In the soft and subtle bends of the kaleidoscope of ever moving moments, you are here.
In the heart-piercing, jagged moments of raw reality, you are here.
In the moments between, where *and* lives, you are here.

Often you go unnoticed.
Often you are taken for granted.
Often you are sought after.

It's in the moments of connection where you live. In perpetuity.

This is the place when eyes, hearts and souls meet.
This is the place where the layers of what divides fade away.
This is the place of what connects beams brightly.

You are the connective tissue of our shared existence.
You are everywhere, everyone, everyday.
You are peace.

Mark Flanigan - USA

Mark Flanigan is a HillVets Fellow in the US House of Representatives. He has served as a National Operations Officer with the International Organization for Migration working to resettle Afghan evacuees across the United States. He was selected to deploy on diverse refugee resettlement assignments to Qatar, Bangladesh, Ecuador, and Costa Rica.

Living Our Ideals

As someone who has been a two-time Rotary Peace Fellow and has dedicated much of my adult life to global peacemaking, I feel quite disheartened with the state of our shared planet today.

Extreme violence, hatred, and injustice are unfortunately more common than ever, while peace and goodwill towards all people seem to be in very short supply. Of all the great possibilities that exist, it seems that humanity is all too often drawn to the very worst of them.

So, what is to be done? Clearly, waiting for positive change is not enough.

While we should certainly petition our elected leaders at all levels, and push national, regional, and international organizations to live up to their mandates, I believe that the best kind of change begins with ourselves and emanates outward. It can also help to stave off the inevitable burnout that comes with frustration over the intractability of injustice.

Thinking globally while acting locally is, in my opinion, the key foundation for a better future through intentional peacebuilding. Starting in one's own personal life, household, and larger community is the best way to center a positive peacebuilding focus that will build concentric circles and influence the world around us. Practicing things like meditation, Yoga, volunteerism, and living a balanced life can help give ourselves a much-needed break while working to change the system from within.

If one looks at the state of the world today, from here in the US and across the globe, it's all too easy to succumb to fear, anger, and despair. As William Lonsdale Watkinson wrote in 1907, *"But denunciatory rhetoric is so much easier and cheaper than good works and proves a popular temptation. Yet is it far better to light the candle than curse the darkness."*

Let us light the candle, breathe deeply, and live our ideals positively in 2025 and beyond.

Nova Jones - USA

Nova Amirah Jones is a 10-year-old girl living in Boston, USA.

Creating a Kind Community

To make world peace you must perform acts of kindness, create a life balance and support our communities.

If we start with ourselves and show positive behavior other people around us may become more positive. For example, be kind. Have a positive mindset, maybe meditate and take deep breaths. We must be kind to ourselves even if we don't feel like it, we can say things to ourselves like positive affirmations. We can learn to ask for help and know we are not alone and show others they aren't either.

You can help others by showing them love and listening to them because they may be struggling. Don't judge a book by its cover meaning don't judge someone by how they look instead of by how they act.

If there are injustices in the world don't stand by and ignore them or take part in it by spreading negative things. We can work together to get rid of violence and make the world a better place to live in. One way to do so is to help those in need, like the homeless. As a community, we can help everyone by helping the environment: reduce, reuse, and recycle. We need less cutting down trees, less destroying animals' homes and less using disposable products.

We can also work together as a community, volunteering to clean our parks and beaches so we can help to keep the animals safe, and so everyone has safe, clean, and happy places to spend time and build peace together in our friendships and families.

We can learn from each other. Let's help each other and the community make the world a better place.

Thank you for listening.

Peter Bevan-Baker - Canada

Peter Bevan-Baker and his wife Ann live in Prince Edward Island where he led the Green Party for over a decade, including the historic result when they became the first Green official opposition in North America in 2019. Bringing an attitude of peacebuilding to politics reflects Peter's lifelong interest and commitment to social justice, environmental protection, and community building. He is slowly extricating himself from politics and aspires to go more placidly amidst less noise and haste.

Think for Yourself and Live for Others

I believe the keys to peace are to think for yourself and to live for others. Let me explain.

For the most part, I am at peace with myself, and what a wonderful gift that is. I call it a gift because it was largely handed to me, this compassionate and level attitude. My greatest privilege in life was to have been raised by caring, kind people in a loving home. I don't take this gift for granted, however, nurturing the fragile core of inner peace with which I have been blessed.

My hope for a peaceful future lies in the knowledge that deep inner peace has astonishing power and allure. People want to feel it, to have it, and most importantly, to share it.

I believe we are here to learn. I find optimism in the belief that empathy and selflessness, which are the foundations of peace, can be learned.

When we discover new and more meaningful ways of being, and share this learning through a life of service, peace permeates our communities. We must also simultaneously unlearn some established ways of thinking and being.

I have spent the last decade of my life as an elected politician. Politics isn't a place that typically promotes or even tolerates peace. Quite the opposite. But with courage and independent thought politicians can be more than the hostile and combative traditions of their parties.

Politics involves everyone, not just those we elect. It's up to all of us to rise above ingrained habits, think independently, seek to understand, and embrace the connections between us.

In short, I believe the keys to peace both within ourselves and collectively, are to think for ourselves and live for others.

Angelo Bernard - Eskasoni First Nation, Canada

In **Angelo Bernard**'s words, "I am from Eskasoni First Nation. I am 24 years old and a father to one. I am a poet, a community-based researcher, and a fisherman. I take great pride in who I am as Mi'kmaq and my rich roots. I am the descendant of Grand Chiefs, poet Rita Joe, a war bride Great Grandmother, and the list goes on. I truly believe the systemic issues that are ongoing in my community cannot be understood without inside experience. It is generations of being stripped from Our Lands, Our Families, Traditions, and Our Tongues. Imagine having everything taken from you as a child and having to adopt the mannerisms, ethics, morals, and religion of people who abused you. Forced to look up to the Monster. It is a battle. I pray and hope that my Brothers and Sisters across the Nation understand the trauma impact, hold on to cultural strengths, and try to be the difference for Our People. Let's go back to our rich and beautiful roots, the Way of Our People.
Msit No"kma"q (All My Relations)"

Gain From Pain

The heat of the grandfathers with a splash,

is worth all the pain that it brings.

As we sit in the circle we chant,

with the beat of the drum we sing.

As the sweat-keeper drops sage,

The smell spreads with the steam.

I find myself through the rage.

I find myself at peace.

We pray not for ourselves, but for others.

Long life, happiness and health.

Some may ask why we willingly suffer.

The answer is finding myself.

The ripple continues,

but strength is within you.

Qamaruzzaman A. - Singapore

Qamaruzzaman A. was introduced to the idea that "education is a force to unite people, nations and cultures for peace and a sustainable future" as a 16-year-old student at United World College in Canada. Over the last two and a half decades, as a third-generation educator, he has aspired to live that mission statement. He does that by engaging learners in peace-learning lessons and workshops. When exploring physics and theory of knowledge with students, he designs lessons to educate for peace. He is currently based in Singapore.

www.vibrations.sg

Peace and Secondary Education

We begin learning in utero and our learning ends only when we take our final breaths. We learn from and with our families, communities, and friendship groups. We learn in two realities: physical and digital.

For all of us who are reading this, we have been brought up in societies that have delegated the responsibility of guiding our human development to schools.

Thus, it is easy for us to forget that learning in the formal space (i.e. education) is but a subset of the sum of human learning. Because of this delegation much of our childhood and teenage years are spent in school. Thus, it is an important space to plant peace culture seeds.

What can we learn? We can learn about ourselves, how to thrive in and contribute to community, and those things we need to know to survive in the societies that we are members of.

When mass education was invented, the 'why' led to the 'what' and 'how' of learning in contemporary schools that is geared towards human doing rather than human being.

Betty Reardon described peace education as having a transformational imperative because it can contribute to "a profound, global, cultural change that affect ways of thinking, world views, values, behaviours, relationships, and the structures that make up our public order".

If a school's hidden curriculum is to educate for peace, peace education becomes formative for the individual learner.

We need to pivot from a survival-centric education to a life-centric one; and break away from thinking that the production of homo economicus is education's primary goal.

By providing space-time for students to explore their inner worlds, examine values and attitudes that nurture not just the self and human community, but also all other life forms on Earth, we can begin planting seeds for non-violent, harmonious, just and sustainable co-existence.

Let us bring equality, justice, and peace for all. Not just the politicians and the world leaders, we all need to contribute. Me. You. It is our duty.
-    Malala Yousafzai (Nobel Prize Winner 2014)

Sharon E. McKay - Canada

Sharon E. McKay is an award-winning author of social justice fiction for young adults. She spent time in Afghanistan as a Canadian War Artist (CFA-VET) and currently lives in Prince Edward Island, Canada.

www.sharonmckay.ca

Peace Building, Baby Steps

Her name was Fiona. She came in the night. She was an autumn hurricane who levelled trees, ripped off roofs, crushed cars, and barricaded us into our home. Picture Jean Valjean inside the barricades. That was us.

We slept through the hurricane and awoke to our neighbour Scott's booming voice. "You guys okay in there?" Scott's voice boomeranged around the neighbourhood regularly. He's a high school teacher.

We were indeed 'okay', physically anyway.

Every exit, including the windows, was blocked. Worse, it was dark, black even, and the electricity was out.

"Not to worry, we'll get you out." Scott sounded triumphant. "It may take a while. You guys got wine?" Scott shouted.

"It's 8:30 in the morning, Scott." My husband, who suddenly realized that we should be dead, bellowed through an inched-open window. But then he added in a somewhat resigned voice, "Yeah Scott, we've got wine."

A bevy of buzzsaws ripped to life. It was a beautiful sound.

Buzzsaws and breakfast Chardonnay seldom fit the topic of peacebuilding.

We 'came from away,' (resettled far from home), leaving our sons, our grandchildren, and long, deep, friendships.

We arrived in our late 50s. A difficult time to make new friends in a neighbourhood filled with young families. What did we have to offer?

Pop, wine, beer, hamburgers, steaks, tasty snacks, and mile-long charcuterie boards. Welcoming smiles.

We threw deck parties and Christmas parties. We bought cookie dough, coupon books, and plants from door-knocking, fund-raising children. We handed out the best treats on Halloween.

We supported all local charities and politicians.

We laughed a lot. We grew younger. Children were back in our lives.

It was not a one-way street. Pies, muffins, and cookies appeared in our kitchen. (Our doors were open.)

"Dad made an extra cake," and "Mom wanted you to try her lasagna," were regular decrees from the front door or the kitchen.

When Fiona hit, an entire neighborhood, including children, were called to action. Limb by limb, branch by branch, we were dug out.

Want to be safe? Know your neighbours.

Want to be happy? Know your neighbours.

True, not all neighbours will be neighbourly, but be neighbourly anyway.

Reach out. Do not sit in your house and wait. Only by communicating do we find connection. ALL peacebuilding comes down to talking to each other.

Want to save the world? Get to know your neighbours.

But there is something more important at work here and it's the children.

They are watching. They are listening.

Chapter Three: Transforming Society

You never change things by fighting the existing reality. To change things, build a new model that makes the existing model obsolete.
- Buckminster Fuller

As a psychologist I have been trained to ask questions such as, "Why does this problem exist in this person's life, the community, or in our societies?" or "What happened to you?" or "What is the cause underlying the symptom?" These questions invariably lead us to more questions, to dig deeper still, to identify the "causes of the causes".

It takes courage for people to engage in the process of change in their lives. They seek to find more contentment, happiness, freedom, safety, health: peace. They seek substantive or transformational change. It is true with groups, communities, and societies.

Peacebuilding, by definition (my definition and that inherent in the principles of a Culture of Peace and the concept of Positive Peace) transforms systems - structural, institutional, political, and societal.

We know that sustainable security, safety, health, and yes, peace, comes only when we engage change strategies at the cause level. For example, we know poverty is the greatest predictor of ill health, and we know that health, gender, and economic inequities are predictors of systemic insecurity and vulnerability to conflict. So, to eliminate poverty is to contribute to peace

I work locally to influence public policy changes with the goal of transforming the way we respond to the challenges facing our societies. Locally and nationally, we introduce, educate, and lobby policymakers, civil society actors, and the public regarding the need for transformational change; change that, by tackling the causes of inequity and vulnerability, will create a resilient, safe, and healthy society for all.

This is peacebuilding.

We have frameworks, such as the Social Determinants of Health (SDH) and the Sustainable Development Goals (SDG) which are based on the understanding that if we address the inequities in our societies and systems- as identified in these frameworks - we can bring peace, wellness, security, resilience and hope universally. These frameworks provide road maps for a way forward through transformational change.

The peacebuilders who offer their thoughts in this chapter are tackling some of the most entrenched 'causes of conflict' in our societies: racism, genderism, ableism, economic and health inequities, colonialism, and capitalism.

They offer us tools for transformation: dialogue, understanding, cultural exchange and learning, universally inclusive policies, curiosity and listening, universal human rights and dignity, and considering the collective over the individual.

...as long as there is injustice somewhere, there cannot be sustainable peace anywhere. We have the duty to improve the quality of life of all citizens and free the potential of every person to build a resilient society and united nation where all thrive.
- Palesa Musa, anti-apartheid activist, South Africa.

Stevie Wills - Australia

Stevie Wills is a performance poet, public speaker and writer. She advocates for the inclusion and empowerment of people with disabilities. Stevie is an associate of CBM Australia who works to end the cycle of poverty and disability.
www.cbm.org.au

Peacebuilding Builds Inclusion and Access for All

Peace, a synonym of flourishing...wellbeing. Holistic, interconnected wellbeing. The well-being of every entity contributing to and dependent upon the well-being of every other entity. Shalom. The flourishing of a person flowing, giving into surrounding lives, community.

Poverty chokes this peace. In low and middle-income countries one in five of those poorest live with a disability. Poverty and disability; interacting, mutually exacerbating disadvantages. The lack of access to employment, education, healthcare and social participation for people with disabilities stifles their peace.

Peace is being seen and understood. Known as an integral member of the community. Peace holds a place for each person to take and flourish, contributing their unique skills, talents and knowledge to the community.

As a person living with a disability in Australia, a fair portion of this peace is mine. I didn't know of the stifling of peace for people with disabilities in low and middle-income countries until I volunteered for CBM Australia.

I was compelled to advocate...to peacebuild. I was welcomed into CBM Australia, an organisation that builds a peace that breaks the cycle of poverty and disability.

Peacebuilding is building access to all aspects of society.

Implementing access into the physical environment. Ensuring variations in communication; braille, sign language, information easy to read, and understand. The writing of peace into laws and policies; mandating inclusion and access. Writing the esteem and value of each person into the common language of communities; erasing all discrimination and stigma.

Peacebuilding recognizes the individuality of individuals and the need for the perspective of each one to inform the implementation of their access and inclusion. This peace: may we build it into communities across the world.

Maciej Witek - Poland/Japan

Maciej Witek is a Rotary Peace Fellow at the International Christian University Peace Center in Tokyo, Japan. Originally from Tarnów, Poland where before starting the fellowship, he worked for a local NGO supporting children and foster families, including families of refugees who arrived in Poland from Ukraine in early 2022. He founded an intercultural education project Global Society – aiming to create opportunities for representatives of different cultures to interact and learn from each other. Since April 2024 Maciej has served on the board of directors of the Global Peacebuilding Association of Japan, an NGO supporting academic exchange and dialogue between scholars and peacebuilders in Japan and around the world. Maciej is also a member of Mediators Beyond Borders International and Empathy Surplus Network USA.

Peace as a Dialogue

To find a way of bringing peace to our world, we should first ask ourselves what peace truly means to us. Is it simply an absence of conflict? Is it cooperation? Does it come with some specific achievement or end goal?

A critical aspect of building peace is dialogue. Dialogue is a conversation, a verbal exchange, which is in contrast to views and situations in which peace projects are based on one voice, one presenter, and conducted in a monological manner. Peace will not be built through monological action.

As well, when we think of peace as a goal or a point, we are suggesting that there is an expected end result, or zenith. The image of peace as a pursuit of a specific goal implies only one correct way of solving the world's problems. That approach lacks consideration of complex identities and histories, as well as diverse sets of cultural norms around the world, and requires the acceptance that one system, or one solution, is superior to all others. These solutions will not be sustained because ultimately, they lead to limiting the voices that could potentially contribute to further improvements.

Through action based on only one voice or perspective power and control are only strengthened which increases the risk of increased structural violence.

Dialogue, on the other hand, takes into account additional aspects such as non-binary thinking and relationality which creates more sustainable solutions.

Instead of looking for one finite and concrete solution, we start rethinking the meaning of peace and accept that it is a constant process - there is no end to peace, no final idea, and no solution to solve all problems.

As peacebuilders, we can encourage and provide opportunities for dialogue not only at the international level but also in our communities, that will encourage consistent rethinking, reimagining, and reinventing how to sustain peace.

Through promoting global education initiatives that teach peace, conflict resolution, and cultural understanding, we can contribute to the creation of inclusive community spaces that foster dialogue and cooperation among diverse groups.

Peacebuilding does not start at the government level but in our neighborhoods, therefore supporting local peacebuilding initiatives and grassroots organizations is crucial.

A peace education will develop empathy, emotional intelligence, and nonviolent communication skills. It is the first step in introducing inclusive policies and practices in workplaces, and schools. Awareness and open-mindedness gained through education will allow us to fully participate and embrace the dialogue, and the constant peacebuilding process.

Maria Julia Moreyra - Argentina

Maria Julia Moreyra is a lawyer and a magister in International Relations. She currently works for the Ministry of Women and Diversity for the province of Buenos Aries, where she is a member of the team working to fight human trafficking. She was the regional director for Latin America and the Caribbean for PeaceWomen Across the Globe and is an expert in Women, Peace and Security. Maria Julia is a Rotary Peace Fellow and Positive Peace Activator.

Peace Will Make Us Free

In recent years we are witnessing a context where human beings have become individualistic, where empathy seems to have given way to indifference to the pain that millions of people suffer. In addition, values and principles are compromised and are in crisis, which is extremely serious.

In my opinion, this leads to peace being in danger. The international armed conflicts that are taking place have the strongest impact on the civilian population. There are efforts at the international level to ensure that peace prevails, but humanity is still witnessing how other human beings have their fundamental rights violated or tragically lose their lives.

Mahatma Gandhi's famous and historic phrase comes to mind: "There is no way to peace, peace is the way."

As a peacebuilder, I always look for ways in my community that lead to peace. This will then have an impact on society at large and so on to higher levels.

A turning point in my role as a peacebuilder was becoming a Positive Peace Activator, thanks to Rotary International's partnership with the Institute for Economics and Peace. Discovering the concept of positive peace, which takes into account the structures and institutions of a society, and which pays attention to resilience, is a very valuable tool to be able to first understand the importance of peace and then to develop activities that lead to peace.

Within the concept of positive peace and its pillars, I firmly believe that some pillars, such as the Acceptance of the Rights of Others and Good Relationships with Neighbors, constitute fundamental bases upon which to achieve inner peace and peace with the beings that surround us.

Not all peacebuilders have the opportunity to be in important positions in international organizations that allow them to have a global impact. But we must always begin to promote peace from our own communities and in every opportunity that comes our way. Whether at a national, regional or international level, we must strive to make the world a peaceful place and this will be the legacy for new generations.

To move forward and strengthen peace, I believe that we must put aside our individual interests, be more empathetic, and return to our roots, away from everything that today does not enable us to focus on the welfare of humanity.

The world is our home, and it is our duty, especially as peacebuilders, to take care of it and make it a hospitable place for all.

Julie Pellissier-Lush - Epekwitk, Mi'kma'ki

Julie Pellissier-Lush is a Mi'kmaw storyteller, photographer, actor, drummer, best-selling author, and the first Indigenous Poet Laureate for Prince Edward Island (Epekwitk). Through her books, songs, poetry and other creative pursuits, Julie celebrates and shares the powerful stories of the Mi'kmaq on PEI. Julie is a cultural teacher and knowledge keeper. She finds inspiration from her elders, as they bravely share their stories, and from today's courageous youth who are embracing and celebrating their rich culture. She is the recipient of the Queens Jubilee, Meritorious Service, and the Senators 150 Medals.

Peace and Reconciliation

Many people have asked for an explanation of what reconciliation is, and every time I am at a different place in my life the answers have always been with what I see at that very instant. In my humble opinion reconciliation is the relearning of past relationships to create new partnerships and friendships, and the older I get the more I see it as a process rather than an actual event, policy, or law. It is like education, young children do not start in grade eight, they start in kindergarten or preschool, they learn the tools they need and then move up a grade.

Reconciliation is much like that, a continued progression not to forget the past, but to learn from it and do better. I have seen so many in this county slowly opening the doors to understanding and learning. They are welcoming the elders to share the knowledge, including inviting the youth to participate, and knowing that we are not what their parents and grandparents grew up learning about us. We are so much more.

Once we get to the point where we can learn from, respect, and understand each other, then we can come to know what peace means: it is where no one is higher or lower than another, where no one is considered greater or lesser than another, where we are equal.

Now, this has taken many years of thinking, observing, learning and gathering knowledge from the world around me.

I am not an elder yet, but as I age I realize why our elders have always had such value. They hold the knowledge from all the experiences they have lived through. I go to my elders often for their wisdom and guidance. They hold the teachings and lessons from generations past and share it with us, so we can use it when we are making our decisions to move forward in a good way.

Does it take work to create change? Absolutely, it really does. A good friend of mine was not ready to think of reconciliation until they read a book by someone they respected as a person; this was a book of a residential school survivor. In those words, my friend learned that they really didn't know about who we are as Indigenous people, and why perceptions and misrepresentations of us must change to create some sort of equality.

Find your person who will help you start this journey, know that it will not be easy, and know that through reconciliation we can find peace and belonging. Something we all need, with the world the way it is now, and maybe how it has always been.

It has taken centuries to get us where we are today, and it will take time for true and meaningful reconciliation to come. We each have enough struggles and hardships, but we can learn together and share with each other, so that in the end, we are all equal.

Oliver Batchilder - Canada

Oliver Batchilder is a 4th-year university student studying Philosophy, Politics, and Economics. His most recent work focuses on assessing food insecurity in rural communities, building on his experience working with organizations supporting individuals facing poverty, homelessness, and other socioeconomic challenges. Oliver is passionate about fostering meaningful change through dialogue, amplifying the voices of individuals with lived experience, and grounding solutions in evidence.

Fostering Understanding and Cooperation

Conflict is an inevitable part of achieving and maintaining peace. Societies evolve and progress through the resolution of tensions, not in the absence of them. The challenge lies not in the existence of conflict itself but in how we choose to address and resolve it. Instead of fostering understanding and cooperation, approaches that exclude those most affected by conflict often exacerbate divisions and lead to further instability.

We operate under the assumption that resources—whether material, emotional, or social—are limited, leading to a constant drive to acquire more, do more, and secure more for ourselves. This mentality, driven by fear of an uncertain future, has historically led to immense suffering and is what has ultimately led to most of the instability in our world.

When individuals and nations act out of a fear of scarcity, they often resort to competition, aggression, and exploitation. While we cannot entirely prevent the scarcity of resources and the desire of others to pursue them, we can find a way to channel our own energy in a direction which opposes this constant materialistic drive for more, while also ensuring that our innate, individualistic tendencies can be directed towards something greater.

Many of us already possess much more than we need, yet we continue striving for more. To provide for yourself, your family, and to pursue a dignified life is not greed—it is a fundamental aspect of human freedom. To me, the whole point of peace is to ensure that everyone has the opportunity to pursue this end.

Greed is what occurs when the drive to accumulate resources, power, or wealth overrides our sense of fairness, empathy, and responsibility to others. This kind of unchecked ambition fuels inequality, breeds resentment, and creates divisions that undermine the foundations of a peaceful society. Greed turns the natural and healthy pursuit of a dignified and peaceful life and the mechanisms one can use to do so, into something destructive.

To build a peaceful world, we must recognize the difference between striving for a good life and allowing that striving to devolve into greed. Greed is in conflict with moderation, and inequality with fairness.

We can't work to find peace if we can't connect with the individuals who are in the greatest turmoil as a result of the greed and inequality that exists; ignoring these voices would undermine the entire project. Understanding how our systems, ways of life, and tolerances are failing requires the insights of those who are most affected by these failures.

We must take every opportunity to learn from others and to engage and work with many people from diverse backgrounds, especially those most negatively impacted. One could see this as a moral imperative, but it is also a practical necessity.

Donna Hicks - USA

Donna Hicks is an associate at the Weatherhead Center for International Affairs and the author *of Dignity: Its Essential Role in Resolving Conflict* and *Leading with Dignity: How to Create a Culture That Brings Out the Best in People*.

Honoring Dignity

In my book, *Dignity: Its Essential Role in Resolving Conflict,* I describe dignity as an internal state of peace that comes with the recognition and acceptance of the value and vulnerability of all living things.

Reflecting on the state of the world at this moment in time, we are far from experiencing that level of dignity consciousness. With the seemingly endless war in Ukraine, the ongoing threat of war in the Middle East, and regional conflicts all over the world, we need leaders who know what it means to *Lead with Dignity.* Closer to home, the surging political division in the United States reveals an underlying ignorance of all things related to dignity.

If we understood that the desire for dignity is universal (we all want to be treated as if we mattered) and that when we treat ourselves and others with dignity, we could begin a new way of being together in the world. Our relationships would be grounded in a mutual recognition of our highest common denominator—our shared yearning to be seen, heard, listened to, and understood. This recognition and acceptance of what unifies us, is the roadmap to peace.

What does it look like to make dignity a way of life? My research has uncovered ten ways that people all over the world want to be treated. I call them the ***Ten Elements of Dignity:***

Acceptance of Identity—Approach people as neither inferior nor superior to you; give others the freedom to express their authentic selves without fear of being negatively judged; interact without prejudice or bias, accepting how race, religion, gender, class, sexual orientation, age, disability, etc. are at the core of their identities. Assume they have integrity.

Recognition—Validate others for their talents, hard work, thoughtfulness, and help; be generous with praise; give credit to others for their contributions, ideas and experience.

Acknowledgment—Give people your full attention by listening, hearing, validating and responding to their concerns and what they have been through.

Inclusion—Make others feel that they belong at all levels of relationship (family, community, organization, nation).

Safety—Put people at ease at two levels: physically, where they feel free of bodily harm; and psychologically, where they feel free of concern about being shamed or humiliated, that they feel free to speak without fear of retribution.

Fairness—Treat people justly, with equality, and in an even-handed way, according to agreed-upon laws and rules.

Independence—Empower people to act on their own behalf so that they feel in control of their lives and experience a sense of hope and possibility.

Understanding—Believe that what others think matters; give them the chance to explain their perspectives, express their points of view; actively listen in order to understand them.

Benefit of the Doubt—Treat people as trustworthy; start with the premise that others have good motives and are acting with integrity.

Accountability—Take responsibility for your actions; if you have violated the dignity of another, apologize; make a commitment to change hurtful behaviors.

If we collectively decided to treat each other with dignity, we just might find that elusive feeling of peace that all humans are yearning for. It's a peace that promotes human flourishing. It's a peace that recognizes the human desire to be connected with others and that the fastest way to promote healthy human connection is by honoring dignity.

Wisdom Addo - Ghana

Wisdom Addo is an educator fostering leadership in young people in schools and communities through training on peacebuilding, human rights, conflict resolution, leadership skills, service-learning projects, and community development. He established the PeaceJam affiliate chapters in Ghana, Liberia and Nigeria.

www.wacpfgh.org

Pathways to a Harmonious World

I have witnessed firsthand the transformative power of peace education in our communities. Our mission at PeaceJam Ghana is to inspire and equip young people to become agents of change, using nonviolent approaches to solve global problems. Drawing inspiration from Nobel Peace Laureates, we have implemented programs that empower the youth to foster peace and stability in their societies.

Education for Peace

Education is the cornerstone of peace. We have established peace clubs for youth in Ghanaian schools. Students learn about conflict resolution, empathy, and the value of diversity. Young participants from different ethnic backgrounds engage in role-playing activities to help them understand and resolve conflicts nonviolently. Inspired by our 2011 visiting Nobel Peace Laureate, Leymah Gbowee, known for her nonviolent approach in ending the 14-year civil war in Liberia, our programs ensure that both boys and girls receive equal opportunities to learn and grow. By teaching young people the principles of peace and nonviolence, we lay a strong foundation for a peaceful society.

Promoting Dialogue and Understanding

We also facilitate intercultural and interfaith dialogues to foster mutual respect and reduce prejudices. We organize a series of community forums in conflict-prone areas at which people from different cultural and religious groups engage in meaningful conversations, promoting understanding and reconciliation.

Empowering Youth

Empowering youth is at the heart of our mission. When young people take leadership roles in peacebuilding activities, they develop the skills and resources needed to advocate for peace and implement projects in their communities.

Youth Leadership and Community Service

One of the most impactful elements of our programs is our *"One Billion Acts of Peace Campaign,"* which supports youth-led projects that address local issues such as advancing women and children, alleviating extreme poverty, providing clean water for everyone, conflict resolution, education and community development, ending racism and hate, global health and wellness, human rights for all, non-proliferation and disarmament, and protecting the environment. These projects not only improve community well-being but also instill a sense of responsibility and leadership in the participants.

Leveraging Technology and Media

In today's digital age, technology and media play a significant role in peacebuilding. We use social media platforms to spread messages of peace and counteract hate speech and misinformation. Our *"Digital Peacebuilders"* initiative trains young people in using technology for peace advocacy; creating online communities and campaigns that promote positive narratives. Encouraging media outlets to adopt peace journalism principles is another critical aspect of our work. By focusing on solutions and peaceful resolutions rather than sensationalizing conflict, media can contribute to a more peaceful society.

By taking these actions, we can collectively move towards a more peaceful and harmonious world. Every individual, community, and institution have a role to play in this journey toward peace. At the West Africa Centre for Peace Foundation, we are committed to continuing our work, inspired by the examples of Nobel Peace Laureates, to educate and empower the next generation of peacebuilders.

Sr. Marion Sheridan - Canada

Sr. Marion Sheridan is a Sister of St. Martha in Antigonish, Nova Scotia. She holds a master's degree in Social Work with an Internship in Psychoanalytic Psychotherapy. She was a liaison at the United Nations for 15 years as part of the Sisters of Charity Federation NGO group. Marion worked in Family Agencies and Private Practice in Boston, Toronto, Halifax and other communities in Nova Scotia. Community development was a central part of her ministry wherever she worked. She served in many leadership positions in her Congregation. Agenda 2030 "no one will be left behind" is vital to her vision and mission.

Let There Be Peace On Earth and Let It Begin With Me

"Let there be peace on earth and let it begin with me" is indeed the foundation for peacebuilding of any kind. Is it a difficult one? Absolutely yes! But our fractured world is comprised of human beings who are global citizens, so it is necessary.

Canada signed on to the Sustainable Development Goals in 2015 with Agenda 30 being "No one will be left behind" which implies peacebuilding. Wonderful and politically correct to sign on, but how can each Canadian be sure Canada implements this action with the dignity of each person in policy and legislation? Many groups already try daily to do this. One group which currently needs our wholehearted support is the youth of our world. They are growing up in a milieu where there are few models of how to be peaceful within oneself and share it with our world with respect for the dignity of each human being.

Most young people are willing to engage themselves, but they need us, with our peacebuilding systems, to reach out to them in trust and hope. We can support them along the way in their education, music, world views, dance, theatre, all that makes them who they are. Why could we not help make peacebuilding part of their school curriculum? At one Conference of Youth at the United Nations which I was graced to attend, four groups said, "We are not the future, we want to forge the future with the wisdom of the present elders". A challenge and an opportunity for sure.

A second action we may take involves Peace Poles. There are presently 250,000 peace poles around the world which say, "May peace prevail on earth". Peace poles are an internationally recognized symbol of the hopes and dreams of the entire human family, standing vigil in silent prayer for peace on earth.

We Sisters of St. Martha have had a peace pole for years on our property in Antigonish. We had weekly prayerful gatherings each Wednesday at our Peace Pole and people of all faith traditions came from around the area.

Imagine if countries where Peace Poles exist reached out to their citizens and asked them to gather on a particular day each week. This could raise our awareness of peacebuilding globally. A monumental task? Ah, yes but our fractured world requires doing such tasks!

These words of Kofi Annan help to keep me focused and so I share: "To live is to choose. But to choose well, you must know who you are and what you stand for, where you want to go and why you want to get there." Have hope and be in it for the long haul.

Sima Samar - Afghanistan

Sima Samar is a Hazara woman and human rights advocate, activist and medical doctor within national and international forums, who served as Minister of Women's Affairs of Afghanistan from December 2001 to 2003. She is the former Chairperson of the Afghan Independent Human Rights Commission (AIHRC) and, from 2005 to 2009, United Nations Special Rapporteur on the situation of human rights in Sudan. In 2012, she was awarded the Right Livelihood Award for "her long-standing and courageous dedication to human rights, especially the rights of women, in one of the most complex and dangerous regions in the world". She is a Nobel Peace Prize nominee and has been awarded the Honorary Office of the Order of Canada. Her appointment to the United Nations Secretary-General's High-Level Panel on Internal Displacement and the UN Secretary-General's High-Level Advisory Board on Mediation in 2019 underscores her significant contributions to global humanitarian efforts. Her journey from a medical practitioner to a powerful advocate for justice and equality is both inspiring and emblematic of the resilience of the human spirit. Her memoir, *Outspoken: My Fight for Freedom and Human Rights in Afghanistan*, provides a poignant account of Afghanistan's past and its present. Currently, Dr. Samar serves as a fellow at The Fletcher School through the Scholars at Risk program, where she continues to enrich the community with her expertise and insights into pressing human rights issues.

Peace is Human Rights, Equality, and Dignity for All

Peace for me is where people live with dignity and rights regardless of their gender, skin color, language, religion, ethnicity and geography. Peace is possible only if we implement the norms and principles of human rights and equality for everyone, everywhere, and all of the time.

First, peace must have at its foundation gender equality, which begins with meaningful participation of everyone at home without discrimination against female family members. The absence of gender equality in the family promotes discrimination and germinates the seeds of conflict in society.

Second, we must focus on quality education everywhere, and education from a human rights-based approach. We need to train the young generation to have a strong belief in human rights and equality.

Third, the rule of law in a nation and globally is essential to sustainable peace.

The law should protect freedom, human rights and dignity of the people, rather than restrict people's freedoms and rights. The world should be run by rule of law, not by the rule of military power. Accountability and justice should apply to everyone without any exception.

Fourth, peace depends upon the inclusion of women substantively in all governing bodies and in the peace process.

Peace is not silence at the point of a GUN. Peace should be measured by human security from fear and wants!

Somia Sadiq - Canada

Somia Sadiq is the founder of Narratives, an award-winning practice based in Canada focused on Impact Assessment and Conflict Transformation and Kahanee, an international non-profit organization focused on stories and storytelling for peacebuilding.

www.narrativesinc.com   www.kahanee.ca

Weaving the Fabric of Peace

Peacebuilding requires bringing together stories, identities, and knowledge systems in ways that honour the collective while celebrating the uniqueness of human experience. Peace is like a beautiful fabric, threads interwoven in intricate patterns and beautiful colours, strengths, and textures. To be our fabric of peace requires the following:

Space to honour identity expressions: In any conflict, unless people are feeling seen and heard, it is unlikely for them to feel respected. Any approach to peacebuilding efforts must then honour peoples' ways of expression; is music how they express, is it songs, is it in story, is it through gathering around food? Is it in how they listen to stories, how they carry stories in their blood memory? Taking the time and creating space for people to express in ways familiar to them can go a long way to build peace processes that are sustainable.

Space to honour ancestral systems: In any conflict, unless people can find some aspect

of the resolution process that pulls on a cord tied to their own identity, it's challenging to find fairness in that process. If I grew up observing, participating, celebrating dialogue-centric, story-centered approaches to resolving conflict, any resolution efforts that don't have these elements are unlikely to feel fair. We need to create space to honour ancient, ancestral approaches to conflict transformation.

The use of trauma-informed approaches: Peacebuilding efforts must be rooted in trauma-informed approaches. This requires understanding the role of trauma in conflict, how trauma impacts how people participate in peace processes, and building a process that incorporates principles of awareness and acknowledgement; physical, cultural, and psychological safety; trustworthiness and transparency; empowerment, choice, and control; and collaboration and mutuality.

Critical self-examination: As peacebuilders, we must continue to reflect on our own privilege, our place, and our role. Are we starting to sit in echo chambers where we no longer question our own positions? Are we only engaging in conflicts that are comfortable to engage in? Worse yet, are we shying away from engaging in peacebuilding efforts where our own countries, communities, or societies may be at fault? Are we starting to forget who we are as peacebuilders?

Ongoing learning, questioning, and wondering is critical for peacebuilders to be able to continue to play the role we all committed to in our journey to make the world a better place.

Ellie Kisyombe - Ireland/Malawi

Ellie Kisyombe, is a founder, mother, activist, and political candidate. In 2015, Ellie co-founded an Irish Café Award-winning social enterprise called OurTable with fellow activist and chef, Michelle Darmody. In 2019 Ellie was the first asylum seeker to run for the local election. Ellie is originally from Malawi and experienced living in the Direct Provision system for many years in Ireland. Ellie has also spent many years volunteering with the Irish Refugee Council working on the campaign to end Direct Provision and was a key participant in public outreach and awareness-raising activities.

Embracing Diversity, Building Bridges: A Path to Global Peace

As we strive for a world where peace reigns, it is imperative that we acknowledge the profound impact of cultural differences on global harmony. The collective community can bridge this gap by embracing diversity and inclusivity, fostering a culture of understanding and empathy. Embracing diversity, with a specific focus on migrants, refugees, and asylum seekers is a crucial step towards achieving global peace.

The influx of members of these communities into new societies presents an opportunity for cultural exchange and understanding. These individuals, often forced to flee their homes due to conflict, persecution, or hardship, bring unique perspectives and strengths to their new communities. By welcoming and integrating them, we enrich our societies and promote cross-cultural understanding. However, this requires a concerted effort to address the challenges they face, such as language barriers, cultural adjustment, and discrimination.

It is, therefore, essential to implement initiatives that promote language training and cultural orientation programs for newcomers. Interfaith dialogue and community events can also play a vital role in fostering understanding and breaking down stereotypes.

Furthermore, supporting education and job training initiatives for migrant and refugee communities can empower them to become active contributors to their new societies. Advocating for inclusive policies and legislation is also crucial in ensuring their rights and dignity are protected.

Celebrating diverse traditions and heritage through cultural festivals and events can also help to promote cross-cultural understanding and appreciation. By recognizing and valuing the diversity of our global community we can break down barriers and create a foundation for peace. However, it is important to acknowledge that embracing diversity is only one aspect of achieving global peace. We must also address the root causes of migration, such as conflict, poverty, and political oppression, by supporting sustainable development and humanitarian efforts globally.

Through inclusive policies, education, and cultural exchange, we can build bridges across cultural divides and create a world where peace is not just a dream, but a reality for all.

Goran Bandov - Croatia

Goran Bandov PhD is a Rotary Peace Fellow, lawyer and political scientist, science diplomat, Full Professor of International Relations and Diplomacy, World Academy of Art and Science Fellow, Global Young Academy Alumni Plus Fellow, Croatian Club of Rome President, Foreign Affairs Committee of Croatian Parliament Member, International Relations and Sustainable Development University Department Head at the University of Zagreb, former Vice Dean at Dag Hammarskjöld University College of International Relations and Diplomacy in Zagreb (2009-2019) and former Research Fellow at the Institute for Peace and Security Studies of the University of Hamburg (2009-2014).

Quality Education: A Prerequisite to Attaining Positive Peace

As a child, I felt the pain of war. I spent months in a basement hiding from bombings and then years as a refugee in a foreign country, separated from my family who remained in the war zone. During those painful times, I made a strong commitment that whatever path I chose in life, it would be one that worked to prevent others from enduring the same suffering that my family, community, and I went through. I held onto this commitment and as a professor of international relations and diplomacy I teach about peace, diplomacy, reconciliation and dealing with the past around the globe.

Contemporary societies are grappling with a series of crises, conflict escalations, climate change, global migration, injustices, corruption, global and regional health challenges, dysfunctional states, and global geopolitical turmoil. Peace has been replaced by wars in many regions of the world. Our urgent reaction is needed.

While each community has its own local priorities, implementing all pillars of positive peace and sustainable development goals is a duty that ensures a high standard of living and protection for all, particularly the vulnerable. Through dialogue, solidarity, trust, strong partnerships, and a sense of global community we can achieve shared solutions and collective progress.

Quality education, as a lifelong process, represents the most effective instrument for ensuring positive peace, sustainability and social progress. It must be based on developing new knowledge and skills, understanding what has been learned, fostering thinking outside the box, creating new ideas, encouraging dialogue and solidarity, as well as learning how to find common ground and achieve win-win outcomes.

Education must be inclusive of all citizens, especially young people, women, vulnerable groups and decision-makers. While teachers and the academic community play leading roles in education, achieving a knowledge-based and prosperous society requires the participation of everyone, especially media and non-governmental organizations.

I am very proud that the Rotary community plays a pivotal role in the field of (higher) education on a global level, particularly in peace studies.

Through Rotary, I have gained many allies in the pursuit of peace, justice and social progress. I have acquired new knowledge, methods, techniques and skills, and shared my own. Although each war and its consequences are unique, they are fundamentally the same. Peace advocates can learn a great deal from one another, especially how to avoid mistakes in the peacebuilding process, how to prevent conflict escalation, and how to achieve positive peace.

We are not a big group of people – but small groups of visionaries were always the ones who changed the world.

Jo Berry - England

Jo Berry is a British peace builder. She founded Building Bridges for Peace in 2009, after losing her Dad in a terrorist attack, with the goal of promoting peace and conflict transformation around the world. She had spent the last 24 years in dialogue with the ex-combatant who killed her Dad. Her reconciliation work was featured in the film *Beyond Right and Wrong* and is studied around the world. Jo is passionate about young people and empowering them to be positive change-makers. She believes everyone deserves a voice and creates safe places for people to be heard.

www.buildingbridgesforpeace.org

Building Bridges for Peace

We are finding a way to create peace in our world. Part of my daily rhythm is working on the belief that peace is possible. To have hope is to be part of a nonviolent force for change.

There is work we can all do. I will start by sharing my own inner and outer work and how this reflects on my perception of the world.

Forty years ago, I chose to bring peace to the nightmare of losing my Dad in a terrorist attack. I decided not to blame an enemy but instead sought to understand why someone would choose to kill. I had no choice over what happened to me, but I could determine how I responded and focus on ending the cycle of violence and revenge.

Twenty-four years ago, I met the man who planted the bomb, Patrick Magee, looked into his eyes and saw his humanity. The first meeting lasted three hours, and later, he would say my empathy disarmed him. For the first time, he realised he had killed a wonderful man with a soul.

Since then, we have met over 300 times and spoken together in public. I now see him as my friend. I didn't meet him to change him but to transform myself. I now know we can hear all sides of a conflict and have unbounded empathy for each side.

There are no enemies, no sides, just people struggling to make sense of their inherited narratives and challenging situations.

I have seen that we all have our humanity, and the work is to remove all internal and external obstacles to knowing this truth. We can still challenge people, but without blaming and shaming. People change when they understand the impact of their actions, when they feel heard, and when someone wants to understand the needs they are trying to meet.

Can we let go of our need to be right and make you wrong? Can we let go of our need to blame and shame? Instead, can we be curious and listen to our 'other'? Can we open our hearts to hear your story?

When we see the humanity of all, when we uphold the dignity of all, and when we can have unbounded empathy for all, then peace is possible.

Peace is possible.

It begins with us.

Some believe it is only great power that can hold evil in check, but that is not what I have found. It is the small everyday deeds of ordinary folk that keep darkness at bay. Small acts of kindness and love.
--- Gandalf, The Hobbit, J.R.R. Tolkien

Krissta Kirschenheiter - USA

Krissta Kirschenheiter feels most at home on islands. Her childhood was spent growing up on the islands of Pohnpei, Federated States of Micronesia (FSM) and on Saipan, the Commonwealth of the Northern Mariana Islands(CNMI). She has directed national and international pro bono legal assistance projects throughout the State of Nevada, the CNMI, the FSM and in the U.S. Virgin Islands. Living and working on small islands has enhanced Krissta's understanding of the everyday impact climate change is urgently having on island communities. Krissta has devoted her career to representing low-income and indigent people in a variety of civil legal matters, including immigration, family law, housing, consumer, public benefits and disaster relief and recovery. Krissta is a Rotary Peace Fellow and is currently the Director of Pro Bono Services for Nevada Legal Services.

Peacebuilding Grounded in Indigenous Knowledge

When I dream about global peace and how we as a society might best attack wicked world problems like war and the climate crisis, it helps me to first remember to ground who I am. I am many things: a mother and a feminist, a lawyer and a peace practitioner. But I am also a second-class American citizen, which means my entire life existence has been framed by this positioning, with all the privileges and unique circumstances it brings me.

Now I am living a new era of my life where I am trying to relearn the entire world's history. I aim to do this by reframing current international and domestic affairs within an enlightened understanding of the Colonial and Christian education of my childhood. Interestingly, it was only two years ago, while studying as a Rotary Peace

Fellow, that I came to realize that my formative years of life experiences, growing and learning alongside Indigenous knowledge, provide me with a unique perspective on world peace.

My earliest life memories begin for me at ages 3 and 4 - growing up on the Micronesian island of Pohnpei. I lived there at a time when the Indigenous peoples had united and declared their independence from the United States but had yet to enter into the Compact of Free Association (which would forever cement dependence on the U.S. going forward, given the strategic location of these island people in Asia Pacific). I was very young, so I learned the Pohnpeian language before my family moved to Saipan, the home of the Chamorro and Refaluwasch peoples.

My ancestors came from Europe, so I am not an Indigenous person. However, it is in the nature of the Micronesian people to accept and teach all humankind, especially children, to be welcomed as family in a way that nurtures belonging and lifelong learning. I was taught from a very young age about spirits, how not to offend them, how to listen to the messages animals bring, to feel nature in a spiritual sense, to feel when the earth is suffering.

You do not question these things, as they are beyond your earthly understanding, you only seek to make the world better in your daily living. Family, and by extension, community, is everything in the Pacific Islands. Without your community, you are often lost, sad, anxious. Knowing that you always have a home in your community helps when you are away. This is all part of Indigenous knowledge.

I was taught many names for peace concepts while studying in Australia, such as slow violence, positive and negative peace, everyday peace. You can put labels on these ways of being, living, striving - being specific about the words you use is a Global North habit. But regardless of what you call peace, I believe there is something to be said about learning to tap more into balancing Indigenous knowledge with your daily living and being.

It will benefit all of humanity to learn more about Indigenous knowledge if we truly want to strive for a more peaceful global community.

Ellen Maynes - Papua New Guinea

Ellen Maynes is a Rotary Peace Fellow who works on gender and inclusion in countries impacted by fragility and conflict. Ellen currently lives in Papua New Guinea where she enjoys some of the best coffee and sunsets in the world.

Building Peace through Dialogue and Conversation

I was backpacking when I saw the graffiti on a wall in Vilnius, Lithuania: an eye for an eye makes the whole world blind. While my home country was never affected by conflict, the things I'd seen in my travels stuck with me, piles of children's shoes at Auschwitz, Sarajevo roses, and the wall dividing Falls and Shankill Road in Belfast.

Today in the news and in my work on gender and inclusion in fragile and conflict-affected countries from Myanmar to Papua New Guinea I see othering, fear, distrust, discrimination, revenge, war against women's bodily autonomy, lives and livelihoods lost. It feels like the world is turning a blind eye whilst thousands of people flee their homes, crossing borders for safety.

While technical elements of peace like agreements, legislation and policy and justice processes are critical, these must be complemented by dialogue to get to the heart of the conflict.

Profoundly difficult and uncomfortable, that dialogue must be human, and community based. Time and time again we have seen how dialogue and conversation make a difference in peacebuilding processes, especially when both men and women are represented. In Bougainville, PNG, women's groups played an important role in peace and reconciliation, walking into the jungle to negotiate with combatants, arranging peace marches, and lobbying for a peaceful resolution.

As I reflect on what needs to change, dialogue and creating mutual understanding and trust are critical. Only with this, can communities recover and move forward. The opposite of an eye for an eye might just be human grace – communities having the courage to seek out mutual kindness and forgiveness and common ground to move past conflict.

Chapter Four: Gender and Peace

I,
The woman,
Not accommodated in the meaning of peace,
Amidst the brutality and power,
Living and surviving species on its own,
On the dichotomy of peace and war,
Searching for historical and transcendent existence.
- Susan Risal, Nepal

Women, girls, and gender diverse people are too often the silent victims of direct, structural, and cultural violence. Through direct violence and brutality, targeted gender-based violence, gender apartheid and femicide, human trafficking and slavery, sexual exploitation, loss of income and food security, or misogynistic policy, women are disproportionately affected by conflict.

In 2021 the World Health Organization reported that almost one in three women across the world have experienced intimate partner violence and/or non-partner sexual violence at least once in their lifetime. Today it is estimated that 70% of the world's refugees are women and their dependent children.

And yet women are vastly underrepresented at peace negotiation and decision-making tables, even though it has been shown that peace that is built with women at the table results in peace that is more successful, equitable and sustainable. The United Nations, with a Women, Peace, and Security agenda, has recognized that women play a key role in post-conflict economic recovery, social cohesion and development, and security and governance. However, in 2023, statistics indicate that fewer women were involved in peace processes than the year before and, during the same period, the number of women dying in conflict increased by 50 percent.

This chapter introduces you to women leading peace throughout the world; journalists who have witnessed the impact of conflict on women and girls, peacebuilders working to build resilient and inclusive communities or who are working on the forefront of conflict zones, women who have chosen to be peacebuilders after experiencing the violence of conflict firsthand, and feminists who are challenging us to consider the women.

We are convinced that strengthening women's leadership at every
level is key to advancing peace, sustainable development and human
rights in the 21st century.
~ Mary Robinson

Mellissa Fung - Canada

Mellissa Fung is a veteran journalist, best-selling author, and award-winning filmmaker. Her latest book, *Between Good and Evil: The Stolen Girls of Boko Haram*, debuted on the Canadian best-seller list for non-fiction in April 2023. Fung has travelled the world producing original documentaries for Al-Jazeera International, the Canadian Broadcasting Corporation (CBC), and TV Ontario, among others. She covered the war in Afghanistan as a field correspondent for the CBC, leading to her best-selling first book, *Under an Afghan Sky*, which chronicled her experience as a hostage after she was kidnapped while on assignment in Kabul in 2008. In addition to Al Jazeera, her work has been featured in The Globe and Mail, The Huffington Post, The Walrus, The Toronto Star, TRT, CNN, and PBS. Her numerous awards include the Gracie Award, the Commonwealth Broadcasting Association award, and the New York Festivals Gold and Silver awards. She holds a master's degree in journalism from Columbia University in New York. She was appointed as an officer to the Order of Canada in 2024.

Peacebuilding Starts with Healing: Women at the Table

Peace feels like a distant dream in June 2024. Israel and Hamas are still fighting, Ukraine is still fighting back her Russian invaders, the Lake Chad region is beset by Boko Haram terrorists, the Taliban have cut off half their population from public life, and that is only a few of the multitude of problems humanity is facing today. These conflicts have one thing in common: intentional, often sexual, violence perpetrated against women. It is the oldest weapon of war, and it continues to be used with impunity because sexual crimes committed in conflict are often the most difficult war crimes to prosecute.

Post-mortem investigations of the victims in the October 7, 2023, Hamas attack in Israel show evidence of some of the most heinous – even deviant – sexual crimes committed on women before the terrorists killed them. A UN report released in late 2023 detailed horrific sexual violence committed by Russian soldiers on Ukrainian women as young as 16 and as old as 83. In Afghanistan, where I spent the better part of two decades covering the progress women were making, they are now living in hiding and fear. Their hard-won rights ripped out from under them when the Taliban returned to power, and the international community has been rendered powerless by a band of bearded men who seem to think that running a country requires the subjugation of women.

I had the privilege of spending several years going in and out of northeastern Nigeria, researching a book and filming a documentary with the survivors of Boko Haram. The shame and stigma with which those women must bear their trauma is unimaginable.

Many have been ostracized by their communities and even their own families. As they opened up about their experiences, they slowly began to reclaim their stories, their history, even their dignity. For some, this was the first time they were able to speak openly about being "married off" to Boko Haram members.

Dr. Fatima Akilu is the pioneering Nigerian psychologist who started a non-profit to help bring peace to that part of her country. She works with both survivors and Boko Haram terrorists who have left the organization. She told me something that stuck with me, since it struck me as so obvious and simple: "If women can't heal from their trauma, this country won't be able to heal."

It's true: if those who suffer the most in conflict – women and children - are not given the space and resources to process their trauma, it becomes a scar that can never truly heal. And in order to ensure they get those resources women must be at the table at peace conferences and cease-fire negotiations. Only they can fully advocate for themselves and perhaps find justice for the crimes committed against them.

To broker a peace that does not include women, and their particular trauma, is to ensure that violence will continue to be used against them and that the oldest weapon in war will remain the sharpest.

Ruth-Gaby Vermot - Switzerland

Ruth-Gaby Vermot, president of PeaceWomen Across the Globe, initiated "1000 Women for the Nobel Peace Prize 2005", a network of female peace activists from around the world. She is a former member of the Swiss Parliament and member of the Parliamentary Assembly of the Council of Europe. On behalf of the Council of Europe, she investigated femicides in Mexico and cases of organ and human trafficking and illegal child adoption in Eastern Europe. She co-authored the Council of Europe Convention on Action against Trafficking in Human Beings and followed up on the implementation of the Convention in various countries.   www.1000peacewomen.org

The Future of the Planet

My dream of a peaceful world without war and violence, where everyone can eat properly, live well, has paid work, leisure time, access to schools and a reliable health infrastructure; where people can think politically and speak publicly with impunity, can move, meet and travel – in other words, a peaceful world – is something I share with millions of people.

When reality sets in – which it always does – the world is full of wars, crime, climatic damage and violence and people are worn down by poverty and hunger and driven by desperate existential fear. Everyday life! It is difficult for me to imagine a vision for the future in the knowledge of the many on-going wars, the horrific threats, the misery of refugees and displaced persons and the false security suggested by armament and militarisation. All of this is a toxic sludge that hampers my steps towards a more hopeful future. And yet, to give up would be to admit that the evil, rotten, destructive and violent things in this world are stronger than the many creative attempts to protect this earth and its people.

We want security! But security today is a purely military term that signifies dangerous arsenals of weapons, sophisticated war strategies, well-stocked armies, and enemies that need to be destroyed. Armed security is unsettling, threatening and wrong. What we urgently need is a security that is based on human and women's rights and is a strong alternative to violent patriarchy. This involves complete disarmament, demilitarisation, a transparent peace economy and, above all, the participation of women in all areas of social and peace work. We need a culture of peace.

PeaceWomen Across the Globe works, for example, with Ukrainian women – those who have fled abroad, those who have been displaced and those who remain at home - since Russia's war of aggression started. At Women's Peace Tables, women have taken an in-depth look at what security means to them. "A good neighbourhood, work, fair wages that are enough to live on, good schools for children and a reliable police force to protect against domestic violence make people safe," say the women. Olena, an economics professor, is even more precise: "The more weapons we get, the less safe we feel."

We want peace! Peace is only possible if women also have a say and play a leading role in shaping it. Leading? We are still a long way from that – even though it has been statistically proven that peace processes that involve women lead to longer-lasting peace.

PeaceWomen Across the Globe was founded to make women's tireless peace work visible and publicly recognizable. Their work is an indispensable basic condition for peace and peaceful societies. It not only makes an essential contribution to the economy, it also constitutes the basis for diligence, solidarity and human dignity.

The participation of women in all phases of conflicts, beyond acts of war and beyond peace resolutions, is indispensable. To get peace processes off the ground requires that everyone has the will to consider peace in the first place and to implement the negotiated terms, even when setbacks threaten. The familiar image of warlords shaking hands after peace agreements is deceptive. There is much delicate work to be done: conflicts must be understood, reconciliation practised, truth-finding addressed and a transitional justice system dealing with war crimes must be established. The dead must be found and buried, losses and traumas must be dealt with. All this is impossible without the participation of the civilian population and especially women. Democratic institutions and fair elections are necessary to enable people-centred, inclusive and rights-based policies. In short, the new societies must offer what people need to live a cared-for, caring and safe life after conflict.

The future of the planet is more fragile than ever with the current 55 theatres of war leaving huge destructive footprints around the world. However, I am convinced that with fearless women who engage in peace processes despite threats, persecution and violence, we can make this future brighter and more livable.

We, the millions of networked women worldwide, are the power that builds peace. Decidedly and absolutely!

ElsaMarie D'Silva is the founder of the Red Dot Foundation (India) and President of Red Dot Foundation Global. She is the co-founder of the Brave Movement, a coalition to end global child sexual abuse, and the founder of Beyond Black, a social enterprise that leverages art for good.
www.reddotfoundation.org

Grassroots Peacebuilding: Local to Global

I work on an everyday conflict that impacts the lives of over 50% of the population - sexual and gender-based violence (SGBV). According to UN Women, one in three women around the world experience some form of SGBV at least once in their lifetime. This violence is experienced more disproportionately by women than by men. Yet 80% of survivors choose not to report it for fear of dealing with the police, bringing shame and dishonour to themselves and their families and the struggle with the lengthy process for justice. As a result, most of these crimes do not make it to official statistics and there is a silence around the issue, normalising these experiences.

Over eleven years ago, there was a horrific incident in Delhi, India where a young woman was gangraped on a bus multiple times and left to die on the streets. Her story inspired many to take to the streets in protest, demanding stricter laws and punishments.

As a survivor myself, I launched the anonymous reporting platform Safecity to crowdsource personal stories of SGBV so that we could understand the scope of the problem. These stories are geotagged and visualised on a map, identifying local patterns and trends of SGBV and opening the door to dialogue, advocacy and identifying solutions for prevention and response.

I have learned through my work that we need to be more aware of what people around us are experiencing. Just because there is a silence around the issue or a lack of statistics, it is not enough.

We have to challenge and confront our biases, harmful gender norms and stereotypes, be active citizens and bystanders and up-skill ourselves with knowledge of the law.

Evidence based data like the Safecity dataset can help in creating space for dialogue in communities where the spotlight is shifted

102

from survivors to the crime/violence. It creates an avenue for building trust within the community, providing much-needed solidarity to survivors, responding to their needs, but also working with institutions to implement policies and laws better.

Safecity started in India but is now a global platform being used by rural and urban communities all over the world. Our partners, who are largely grassroots civil society organisations, have used the data to educate and engage their communities to become more aware of SGBV, identify solutions which have been implemented with religious leaders, education institutions, urban planners, police, city officials and others. Together we have improved the lives of over 1.5 million people in safer cities programming.

Jackie Kauli - Papua New Guinea

Jackie Kauli works in international development and communication for development across Papua New Guinea and Australia. Her work focuses on harnessing process drama techniques, creative practice and communication strategies to contribute to development practice. She is currently a Senior Research Fellow in the Creative Industries at Queensland University of Technology where she mentors doctoral students and staff working in cross-cultural contexts. She is a director with Yumi Sanap Strong Inc. www.yumisanapstrong.org

Women and Indigenous Peacebuilding

Over the past six years, I have been part of a community of human rights workers known as Yumi Sanap Strong (Let's Stand Strong Together), working across Papua New Guinea.

During that time, I have learned much from community-based and women's organisations who have made immense contributions to peacebuilding locally and regionally for many decades. However, most of their work has been invisible and one of the objectives of the Yumi Sanap Strong initiative is to tell their stories and contribute to better understandings of indigenous peacebuilding strategies.

One of these stories has been captured in the recent film Tribal Sisters, which tells the story of Kup Women for Peace, founded by

three women: Angela Apa, Mary Kina and Agnes Sil. The Kup Valley in the Simbu Province of Papua New Guinea was known for sporadic tribal wars since the 1970s. Tribal warfare occurred regularly in the Kup Valley, with men leading warring parties that violently disrupted the lives of women, children and the elderly in the area. In 1999, three women from enemy tribes came together to resolve tribal conflicts and broker lasting peace that ended the violent 20-year conflict.

What they achieved through years of mobilising women in the area was remarkable. The women "used their tears as weapons for peace and through this brought about a process of re-thinking by the men who were involved in the fighting" (Garap, 2004, p. 2)[11].

Today, to maintain peace and curb gender-based violence, the women continue to implement awareness campaigns in the marketplaces and public areas, informing people about their rights and availing their services to those who need help. They speak strongly against tribal fighting, gender-based violence and sorcery-related violence. Many people, especially women, continue to seek counsel and solace from them.

In Papua New Guinea, we face significant challenges in our social and economic development. While our country is rich in resources, this does not translate to development for communities. The colonial influences have disrupted community structures and external influences continue to challenge our identities. Peacebuilding is often seen as something that requires significant external support. And while our state intervention mechanism faces challenges to address issues of violence in communities, community-based organisations have always been instrumental in facilitating dialogue and change in communities.

As a team within Yumi Sanap Strong, we continue to draw on indigenous ways of working to understand and resolve conflicts such as sorcery accusation, violence towards women and children and tribal fighting. We combine indigenous knowledge and arts-based processes and practices including storytelling, drama and filmic approaches to implement peacebuilding processes in communities. If peace is to be achieved, we need to work together as a collective, drawing on each other's knowledge and strengths, and understand and respect that indigenous ways of knowing can contribute to transformative processes of peacebuilding.

---

[11] S. Garap, "Kup Women for Peace: Women Taking Action to Build Peace and Influence Community Decision Making." State, Society and Governance in Melanesia, 2004. http://dspace-prod1.ana.edu.au

Nino Lotishvili - Georgia

Nino Lotishvili is a specialist in intercultural communication and a Rotary Peace Fellow. Coming from Georgia, a conflict-affected area in the South Caucasus, Nino's work in conflict transformation and her own life experience led her to launch two initiatives: NGO ManaTheia Peace Hub and conscious travel company Mindful Georgia, to support conflict-affected communities and individuals throughout Georgia and the South Caucasus region.

Resilient Women Building Peaceful Communities

In multi-ethnic societies people often put up an imaginary boundary line between self and others, developing a number of stereotypes and prejudices about other ethnic groups. Such differentiators can be exploited by political leaders to abuse the concept of culture. This can become an obstacle for civil integration and contribute to the social distance between different ethnic groups within the same territory.

Collective trauma occurs when large groups of people endure widespread and devastating events, such as armed conflicts, natural disasters, or systemic oppression. Unlike individual trauma, which affects a person's psyche and emotional well-being, collective trauma impacts the cultural identity of entire communities. Conflicts, with their profound and far-reaching consequences, exemplify collective trauma by leaving deep scars that shape societies for generations. Unhealed collective trauma can be transmitted unconsciously from one generation to the next, trapping communities in a vicious cycle of violence. Healing these wounds requires a collective effort and a commitment to breaking this cycle and addressing the trauma.

For centuries, women have been at the forefront of efforts to foster peace and stability in their communities, driven by an inner resilience that enables them to navigate significant challenges. This resilience, rooted in emotional intelligence, adaptability, and compassion, is pivotal not only for personal well-being but also for effective peacebuilding.

However, due to entrenched patriarchal norms, these women often feel powerless and marginalised. Their voices are silenced which further deepens a layer of gender-based collective trauma. Such dynamics prevent these women from fully realising their potential in peacebuilding and limit their impact on social cohesion and change.

The need to further empower women, strengthen their resilience and increase their participation in community peacebuilding processes is highlighted by UNSCR 1325, and supported by research I have conducted on the role of Georgian-Ossetian mixed families in reconciliation and peacebuilding. Women represent a crucial natural bridge over hatred and intolerance and are models for positive change in reconciliation processes. However, research also shows that many women feel powerless, and often marginalised.

How can this hidden potential be uncovered and cultivated to support communities in building lasting peace within the context of collective, unhealed trauma? It is essential to focus on developing inner resilience, which enables individuals to reconnect with their deeper pains. As the great Sufi poet Rumi reminded us, "The wound is the place where the light enters you." By engaging with our own wounds, we allow ourselves to reclaim our strength as peacebuilders. In a project that supported and connected women affected by the ethno-political conflicts in Georgia, women were able to share and embrace their painful experiences. By reconnecting with their own feelings and emotions, they were encouraged to remember and rediscover their inner wisdom and self-assertiveness.

As peacebuilding practitioner J.P. Lederach stated, "Social healing is made up of moments of resonance, where voices touch voices in a common space." By fostering a safe environment where individuals can open up, share their experiences, and confront their own pain, they gradually develop greater compassion and empathy for the suffering of others. These qualities—empathy, compassion, and love—are essential for building a sustainable peace.

Susan Risal - Nepal

Susan Risal is a long-term peace practitioner based in Kathmandu, Nepal. She is a Chief Executive Officer of Nagarik Aawaz (Citizen's Voices), a peace-building organization in Nepal which works with conflict-affected youth and women. Susan first became interested in peace-building through her experiences at Nagarik Aawaz. Listening to the many stories of hardship, injustices and suffering of the conflict-affected women made her want to continue her work in peace with commitment and dedication. This led Susan to do a Master's in Applied Conflict Transformation Studies and a PhD in Applied Conflict Transformation Studies so that she could gain theoretical knowledge in peacebuilding, to complement her practical knowledge and contribute that knowledge to improve the lives of conflict-affected people. Susan is very passionate about the issues of conflict-affected communities, particularly the issues of women.

Cry for Peace

The world is grappling with significant conflict and war, resembling the resurrection of World War II. Though the technological aspects are different, the strategies seem similar to those of past world wars, including the annihilation and cleansing of certain communities. It is so disheartening to see the citizens from countries where wars and conflicts are happening, and among them women and children, having to bear the severe brunt of these monopolistic warlords.

The values of being human are in question with the loss of humanity in the countries facing protracted conflict. In this context, it is unimaginable to feel the physical and psychological losses and pain experienced by the citizens of the Israel-Palestine conflict, Russia-Ukraine, Afghanistan, Myanmar, Manipur, Sudan, and many more countries.

We cannot imagine how many generations will have to bear the impact of these brutal wars with the imbalance of the physical, psychological and moral illness at large. However, during these brutal times, people still strive to live their lives, creating sociality, reciprocity, and solidarity, as scholar Roger Mac Ginty highlights in his book *Everyday Peace*.

However, this form of everyday peace power is rarely discussed in peacebuilding work even in times of protracted conflict; nor afterward in the name of the peacebuilding process following the signing of a peace accord. Even in brutal violence, women and children survive by their own means and creativity. The discourse on everyday peace not only fades during a protracted conflict but also when a country enters the peace process.

Examples like Nepal show that structural and cultural violence remains the same, igniting armed conflict. Due to severe pain endured on the battlefield of armed conflict, where their bodies were used as weapons of war to spread the messages of fear in their families and community, many women who experienced conflict-related sexual violence are dealing with losses such as carefree childhoods and dreamy adulthoods. Women's dignity is annihilated and still, the loss continues in the name of prestige for the family and community in this so-called peacebuilding process which is, in its essence, a cold and negative peace.

In any part of the world experiencing crises of war and conflict, women rarely get the space to write their own history. Patriarchy always dominates, and even when it comes to peace accords, asymmetrical power relations among men, women and the LGBTQ+ community play out underneath. When peace processes start, they are celebrated in a big way, but those involved rarely bother to listen to the unimaginable suffering and resilience of women who are also central actors in building peace.

It is commendable to witness, even amid brutality and power, women having the creativity and courage to sustain and protect themselves, their families, and their communities. However, it is also the duty of the state and every citizen to protect and respect the human rights of women and girls, as well as those of the citizens in the LGBTIQ+ community, whereby they can have a carefree childhood, dreamy adulthood and dignified womanhood.

Lisa LaFlamme has been at the forefront of Canadian journalism for over 35 years tackling some of the biggest issues of our time from war zones and natural disasters to the changing political climate around the world. An Officer of the Order of Canada and Order of Ontario, LaFlamme is the recipient of 14 Canadian Screen Awards, including the Gordon Sinclair Award for Excellence in Broadcast Journalism, as well as a Lifetime Achievement Award for journalism. The internationally respected journalist was the first woman to anchor CTV National News, a role she held - as chief news anchor and senior editor - for over a decade. A passionate advocate of democracy, LaFlamme is an ambassador for Journalists For Human Rights, Plan International Canada, volunteers for Right to Learn Afghanistan and is a member of the board of Samara Centre for Democracy.

Nurturing Peace Together

In a world filled with conflict, violence and inequality, peace is a fragile concept that, despite best efforts, seems to be starving for attention. It exists, but only on the fringes of war and concrete solutions are competing with greed, historical grievances and power struggles.

As a journalist, I've spent years covering conflict and subsequent peace talks in various places and almost never are women around that table.

Let's face an irrefutable truth: war is men's work. Always has been. That means half the world's population has no voice on issues crucial to their own survival.

So, what actions can we take now to bring peace to our world? Inclusion would be an obvious and important starting point along with an emphasis on education, not indoctrination.

In the Democratic Republic of Congo, in Afghanistan, in Haiti, in Iraq... in too many places, I've seen that terrible contrast between a mother watching her child sleep on the floor inside an adobe shack, as gunfire cracks and bombs explode in the darkness outside. The mothers I've spent time with have an unspoken contract with a higher power: if we get through this night, tomorrow my children will have peace. But that's a contract rarely kept.

At least 230 million children wake up each day in an active war zone and merely surviving that day is not the kind of education that promotes understanding, empathy and calm coexistence. Instead, it promotes a cycle of revenge.

History tells us the awful truth is that there will never be world peace as long as there are humans and since only humans can cultivate a culture of peace, we have a problem.

I don't have the answers, but I do know that it starts close to home and only by including women in the conversation.

I feel like I've watched civility drain from the public dialogue over the last few years but I'm not willing to give up hope. Instead, I'm willing to believe that the next generation will get it right and restore respect, cooperation and compromise.

If we feed peace, one person at a time, we can watch it grow together.

Chapter Five: Peace in the Midst of Conflict and Crisis

We cannot have peace if we are only concerned with peace. War is not an accident. It is the logical outcome of a certain way of life. If we want to attack war, we have to attack that way of life.
- Johan Galtung

As I write this, I am still in the throes of the hangover from the 2024 US Election results, an election whose tone and rhetoric reflected and stoked division, tension, and fear. It very much felt like an election in the midst of a crisis, or more accurately, a number of crises. Social, economic, and racial division and inequality, women's rights, the climate crisis, gun violence, and more.

As many of the peacebuilders in this book point out, peace is not a point in time, an end goal where we can shake hands and say, "job well done." It is an ongoing process and as crises and conflicts arise peacebuilding needs to have a consistent presence, as well as the flexibility to adapt and change as the circumstances do.

In this chapter, you will read about peacemaking and peacekeeping, as well as peacebuilding. In truth – at least the way I see it – these practices have overlapping scopes and points of intervention. A peacekeeper from Canada speaks of how soldiers on the ground can help communities to establish ways forward that are based in peace. Peacebuilders who have contributed to some of the most notable peacemaking efforts of our time continue their work, offering their experiences to other regions currently experiencing conflict. People fleeing war offer ways to move forward through connection, compassion, and dialogue.

The peacebuilders in this chapter reflect on the challenges of building peace, or at least learning to get along, at times of crises brought on by war, economic insecurity, climate change and environmental degradation, food insecurity, and oppressive and repressive governments. They offer ways to build peace and work toward post-conflict relationships based in reconciliation and the transformation of relationships.

We will not learn how to live together in peace by killing each other's children.
~ Jimmy Carter

Rev. Dr. Gary Mason - Northern Ireland

Rev. Dr. Gary Mason is a Methodist minister and director of *Rethinking Conflict*. Prior to this he spent 27 years in parish ministry in Belfast and played an integral role in the Northern Irish peace process. He holds a PhD in Psychology from the University of Ulster, completed his theological studies at Queens University and has a Bachelor's in Business Studies from the University of Ulster. Gary is an affiliated expert and partner to the Negotiation Strategies Institute, a Harvard University program on negotiation for Israelis and Palestinians and international diplomats. Gary is an international advisor at the European Wasitia Graduate School for Peace and Conflict Resolution at the University of Flensburg in Germany, a visiting academic at the University of Central Florida in conflict transformation, political violence and negotiation, an advisor to the Wolff Institute at the University of Cambridge, and a consultant to the Carter Center in Atlanta, Georgia. www.rethinkingconflict.com

Maybe, Just Maybe: Lessons from Northern Ireland

I was born, grew up and still live in that sectarian cockpit called Northern Ireland, those from the British Unionist tradition call it Northern Ireland. Irish Nationalists many times don't use that word, they call it "the North" or the "six counties". We all understand the power of words, as we have witnessed daily on our tv screens, the violence in the Middle East. Those two divided people do not even agree on the name of what happened in 1948 – Israelis call it the War of Independence and Palestinians the Nakba. Or alternatively, we use words to describe geographical spaces - Israel, Palestine, the West Bank or Judea and Samaria.

And yet I think of people during our conflict on both sides who have taken incredibly courageous steps to cross our political and religious divide, wrestling with the questions of how toxic religion and toxic politics got us into this mess in the first place.

I've seen colleagues, even in the midst of the polarisation in the United States at the moment, see the humanity and the image of God in another person, even though politically, they may not always see eye to eye. And as we despair about the Middle East, and wonder if there is ever any solution, I'm grateful for daily conversations at the moment with both Palestinians and Israelis in the midst of a

114

Palestinians and Israelis in the midst of a bloody war who refused to give up. As a Palestinian friend said to me in the last couple of months, "If we don't do something Gary, we are all doomed." Behind-the-scenes stories may not be making the news on the BBC, RTÉ, CNN, or Fox News yet there's so many individuals, looking for ways forward in very perplexing and difficult situations, and every day when I get up in my home city of Belfast, that has been transformed by our peace process, I know the place is different.

I have hosted over one thousand Palestinians and Israelis in Belfast and Dublin over the last 10 years, looking at lessons from our Irish peace process. It's not a utopia in the space in which I live, but I'm grateful that it is a very different space to the space which I grew up in.

On one occasion when a group of Israelis and Palestinians arrived in Belfast, a young Palestinian woman came up to me and said to me, "Gary, I think this is just a waste of time". In replying to this young woman, I said, "You may well be right, it may be a waste of time, but at the end of the week, I hope you can just say three words to me." She naturally asked, what three words would those be? I replied, "Maybe, just maybe!" That maybe at the end of this week with some of the lessons from the Irish peace process, that maybe you can take

back to your region breathing the oxygen of hope.

The story has a happy ending because the evening before that delegation traveled back to that fractured region of the Middle East, that young Palestinian woman came up to me with tears in her eyes, and said three words, "Maybe just maybe." I'm grateful for the lessons of our peace process as maybe that region of the Middle East, which has a place deep within my heart, that maybe just maybe someday they will be grateful for a completely new beginning.

So, if you ask me if I was to name one key component, and there are a number that were key to the Northern Irish peace process, it has been the role of what I describe as civic society, actually being the social glue that holds our peace process together.

Politicians undoubtedly have a role and an important role, but unless civic society globally begins to move into the public square and shape what are very polarised narratives, our children and our children's children will be wrestling with these problems for generations. So to those who inhabit difficult spaces, can those civic society leaders globally and those who do not feel they even may be leaders, can you create - Maybe just maybe moments to allow future generations to live in a different world?

Aura Hammer - Israel

Born in New York, **Aura Hammer** moved to Israel with her Jewish religious parents and siblings in 1973. She was an architect for many years until she discovered her passion for working for peace during the Second Intifada and her life course changed. She studied facilitation and became a Council facilitator and trainer, working with Jewish-Arab groups, women and educators, working extensively with Itaf Awad, co-founding their organization, Diwan Siti and volunteering with Women Wage Peace and other peace organizations. She also taught and facilitated sustainability to educators. She envisions her life work as helping to create a sustainable future for the next generations, expanding and extending the work to a wider spectrum, including work on eldering and "regenerating society", in order to encompass this vision of possibility.

At the Bottom of My Coffee Cup

Everyday my heart breaks again. I open the news with my coffee and force myself to read how many people died. And I don't understand why they died. Why they remain nameless. I try to imagine them, to pray for their families, for the wounded, for the homeless. I feel helpless each day anew.

I know there is compassion in the world, I know because I feel my own compassion, and I am but one miniscule part of the world. So, what is this evil force that drives men to hate, to killing, to revenge, when it is so clearly not the path to a good happy world, where all can thrive? We have had thousands of years to learn, to perfect ourselves, our ways of life. And still, we make the same mistakes, use the same solutions to the same problems - expecting different results. And the world has become so complex that no one has the solutions anymore. Too many people have given up. If they don't know the answer, then they give up. But it is these people, who know that this way is not the way, who can help us all find the way. We do not have the privilege to give up. We are needed for the change.

How many people are needed if we wish to change this? All of us. How can we become the change we so desperately need? The beginning of change is being open to change. We just need to begin. All of us.

I find that openness to change means first changing myself. To open my awareness of humanity, connection, vulnerability, and personal power.

116

Looking back, I see that allowing myself to feel meant learning how to take off my armor. We create armor to protect ourselves - from society, from war, from personal pain. In the war zone I live in, taking off my armor does not require courage so much as awareness of the fact that keeping our armor on all the time prevents us from connecting to others. It is a barrier which is sometimes necessary, but more often a terrible hindrance. Armor prevents us from seeing and reaching out, creating an impenetrable shell which works both ways. If I was to keep my humanity I needed to feel it.

Taking off my armor was one of my first steps. Rediscovering connection to others followed. Finding my personal power and keeping it is a work in progress. It includes discovering and using my voice, acknowledging the experience, and the wisdom, I gather as I go. But mostly it is staying constant to my belief in our ability as the human race to rise to the next step of our development, the place where we know in our bones that connection is our true humanity, not cleverness, not invention, but knowing how to be connected to all, to sustain and replenish the connections both to our human race and to all life.

And so, every morning I allow my heart to break open again. I persevere in my vulnerability. I hold my coffee in one hand, I hold my broken heart in the other.

George Kimani - Kenya

George Kimani has a PhD in Political Science and Peace Studies from Bradford University, a master's degree in Peace Studies and Political Science from Atlantic International University and a bachelor's degree in Communications (Public Relations) from St. Paul's University. He has worked with International Non-Governmental Organizations and National Non-Government Organizations for 5 years in Senior Management at national (Kenya, Sudan, South Sudan, Somalia, Burundi and Uganda), regional and international (Thailand, Nepal, India, and Myanmar) levels. George has managed diverse and multi-sectoral programmes in the areas of livelihood, health, governance/advocacy, refugees, food security and disaster risk reduction. He has certifications in leadership, theology and Bible studies, refugee protection, monitoring and evaluation, project design, peace and conflict resolution, and disaster management. He is a Rotary Peace Fellow and currently resides in Kenya.

Pathways to Peace

Achieving enduring peace in our world, and particularly within Africa, necessitates a comprehensive and nuanced approach that addresses the intricate root causes of conflict while fostering sustainable development.

Central to this endeavor is the establishment of inclusive governance frameworks that ensure representation and participation from all societal segments, including marginalized groups. Strengthening democratic institutions, ensuring transparency, and rigorously combating corruption are fundamental steps towards this goal.

Tackling poverty and inequality must be prioritized as a cornerstone for peace. In this way, we can mitigate the socioeconomic disparities that often serve as catalysts for conflict.

Strategic investments in education, healthcare, and infrastructure are imperative, as they not only enhance the quality of life but also generate opportunities that contribute to societal stability.

At the community level, grassroots initiatives and local leadership are indispensable in mediating conflicts, promoting reconciliation, and building intergroup trust. The empowerment of women and youth in peacebuilding processes is crucial, given the disproportionate impact on them from conflicts and their inherent resilience and innovative potential in crafting solutions.

Global cooperation is essential. In Africa, the international community must support African-led peace initiatives through financial aid, technical expertise, and diplomatic backing, all while respecting the sovereignty and contextual specificities of African nations.

Immediate actionable steps include fostering dialogue among conflicting parties, supporting disarmament and demobilization efforts, and investing in post-conflict reconstruction.

By integrating these measures with an unwavering commitment to justice, equity, and human rights, we can chart a path towards a peaceful and prosperous future for Africa and the broader global community.

Grace Van Zyl - South Africa

Grace Van Zyl is a Financial Life strategist and currently a member of the Rotary Club of Johannesburg, South Africa. She serves as Community Service Chair and Peace Chair for her district and is also the CEO of The Foundation for Southern Africa Rotary Clubs (FSARC). She is passionate about building the capacity to create positive sustainable peace and presents to Rotary Clubs all over the world on how they can incorporate peacebuilding in their projects. Grace is the current (2024-25) Chair of the Rotary Action Group for Peace.

Intentional Peacebuilding

Growing up in South Africa, peace is more than a concept—it is a daily pursuit woven into the fabric of resilience, reconciliation, and hope that defines us as a nation. Our history is one of profound struggle and transformation, marked by the courage of those who envisioned a country where diversity is our strength and unity our goal. Yet, peace remains a living, breathing endeavour—a process of constant rebuilding, nurturing, and reimagining as we confront new challenges in a rapidly changing world.

Growing up in South Africa during the apartheid era, my earliest memories of peace—or its absence—are tangled with confusion and quiet tension. I remember the siren sounding at sunset, signalling that certain people were no longer permitted on the streets, and I remember seeing separate parks and facilities, designated for "White" and "Black" people. As a child, I couldn't grasp why these barriers existed, but they lingered in my mind as silent questions about what made us different, and why it mattered.

As I grew older, my understanding of apartheid deepened, but the reasons behind this enforced separation and systemic discrimination still eluded me. I came to see the pain and generational scars apartheid inflicted, scars that ripple through our country even today. These wounds of division and injustice continue to fuel racism and inequality, embedding themselves in our institutions, communities, and psyche.

In South Africa, peace is not the absence of these challenges—it is the courageous commitment to confront them. Peace means reckoning with the past while forging pathways of hope and healing, even when the journey is hard. True peace is the commitment to actively address the wounds of inequality, violence, and systemic hardship that have shaped our communities. It is an unbreakable promise to create safe, inclusive spaces where every voice is heard and valued. From the informal settlements to the centres of governance, the call for peace resonates, reminding us that sustainable peace can only emerge through social justice, economic empowerment, and educational access for all.

As the chair of the Rotary Action Group for Peace 2024/2025, I carry this perspective with me. I am inspired by those who, despite past suffering, work to mend divisions and build resilient communities rooted in justice. Rotary's commitment to Positive Peace aligns with our South African vision: a peace grounded not merely in coexistence but in mutual upliftment, justice, and opportunity for all.

My hope is that these efforts encourage others to become intentional peacebuilders, fostering unity and understanding not only in policy but in hearts, minds, and daily lives.

Debi Parush - Israel

Debi Parush is a PhD candidate in Environmental Sciences at the University of Haifa, Israel and has a certificate in conflict resolution from Carleton University in Ottawa, Canada. She co-founded Children Inspiring Peace, an initiative that brought children together to explore peace from different cultural perspectives, was active in Women Wage Peace and Potlucks for Peace, and worked at the aChord Center - Social Psychology for Social Change and at the Canadian Nuclear Safety Commission.

An Inclusive Process for a Better Future

Facing the threats of war, we may overlook well-known tenets. This list has been compiled from recent research on resolving wicked problems and fieldwork in peacebuilding. As a checklist, it can help identify gaps and opportunities for more effective decision-making and conflict resolution.

Are the latest developments communicated at all levels, top-down and bottom-up?

If not, we risk replacing old problems with new ones. For instance, if a national goal changes and the regional offices are unaware, new issues could emerge.

Ensure information sharing across all levels of leadership, replacing "tugs of war" with collaborative dialogue involving governing bodies and civil society.

Do all stakeholders understand each other's rules of engagement?

If not, clashes might escalate into conflicts. For example, overlooking community values when negotiating with an individual could fracture the community and undermine the negotiation.

Foster awareness of diverse values and rules. Promote clarity and fairness in rule enforcement to build trust and maintain confidence in the system.

Are individuals or groups being held accountable for their own actions, or are entire groups blamed?

Attributing one person's actions to a wider group can escalate conflict.

Focus accountability on individuals who break rules instead of treating an entire group as the enemy to prevent unfair generalizations and reduce tensions.

Are the greater good and individuals' rights balanced appropriately?

An imbalance could lead to distrust and system breakdown.

Listen to concerns from all stakeholders and address them sincerely and incrementally to ensure that improvements benefit everyone without harming others.

Is there a structured, safe space for parties to engage?

Without safe spaces for dialogue and resolution, issues may remain unresolved, increasing tension.

Establish and enforce structured spaces where participants can safely and fairly raise issues and mitigate disputes constructively.

What mechanisms are in place for enforcing rules of engagement?

Words alone may not always suffice in volatile situations. At times, strength may be necessary for enforcement. This should be paired with respectful communication.

Ensure appropriate enforcement mechanisms are available, blending strength with mutual respect and hope to de-escalate conflicts and build understanding.

Are benefits being shared fairly?

Unfair distribution of benefits can lead to unsustainable outcomes, regardless of whether change occurs through force or dialogue.

Guarantee equitable sharing of benefits to ensure lasting results and prevent grievances.

What messages and actions convey a commitment to a better common future?

Sharing hopeful visions and demonstrating readiness to collaborate can replace conflict with dialogue, fostering trust that leads to resolving issues collectively.

Communicate mutual commitment to a better shared future, emphasizing practical actions that address everyone's needs.

On a personal note... Being a Canadian living in the Middle East, with its cultural diversity and history of conflict, has shaped my reflections on peace. I wonder whether historical tensions between French, English, and Indigenous peoples have truly been resolved or simply well-managed on a foundation of evolving best practices and tenets. My hope is that these pragmatic, respectful solutions may result in getting along and lead to a sustainable peace globally.

Joanna Nakabiito - Uganda

Joanna Nakabiito has experience in preventing violent extremism and terrorism, youth violence prevention, disarmament, and peace research. She is also participating in the global campaign against Lethal Autonomous Weapon Systems and their implications for the protection of civilians in armed conflict. Joanna is a postgraduate finalist in MA Peace and Conflict Studies at Makerere University and has a podcast, "*The Peace Pod with Joanna Nakabiito*" where she discusses the theoretical, practical and conceptual dimensions of conflict, and provides recommendations for conflict prevention programming.

Laying the Groundwork for Peace

To find a path to peace for our world, our communities, and our societies, especially in areas where civic space is repressed, we must focus on building resilience and fostering education for empowerment. These actions, which can be initiated immediately, lay the groundwork for peace even in environments where expression and participation are restricted.

First, we need to nurture community resilience by encouraging informal networks of support and solidarity. In many repressive settings, formal avenues for advocacy and assembly are closed off, but communities often find alternative ways to connect. Through small, localized actions—such as neighborhood gatherings, informal support groups, and trusted spaces like religious centers— people can share information, support one another, and foster unity. These networks don't challenge authority directly but create safe, nonviolent channels for collaboration and mutual aid, building the trust needed to navigate restrictions together. In repressed communities, resilience becomes a quiet yet powerful form of resistance, ensuring that when civic space eventually opens, people are ready to engage constructively and peacefully. By nurturing these networks, we lay a foundation for societies that can withstand division and oppression, moving closer to sustained peace.

Education for empowerment is the second essential action to foster peace, equipping individuals with the knowledge to advocate peacefully and responsibly. In many repressed societies, education is often limited or controlled, with little focus on critical thinking, civic awareness, or rights-based learning. By prioritizing informal education that emphasizes empathy, conflict resolution, and civic responsibility, communities can empower their members, even under restrictive regimes. Community workshops, storytelling sessions, and digital resources that promote human rights and nonviolent advocacy can transform individuals into informed, engaged citizens. Such education lays the groundwork for peaceful, informed participation and encourages people to seek justice without confrontation, fostering peace over time.

To move toward a peaceful future, humanity must prioritize these actions. By nurturing resilience and empowering through education, we create a society prepared for peace—even in the face of repression. These steps don't just address immediate needs; they cultivate the deeper social change needed for lasting harmony across our communities and societies.

Nabil Oudeh - Canada

Nabil Oudeh was born into conflict. As a Palestinian growing up in Israel, Nabil experienced the impact of conflict on all aspects of life. As a teenager, he challenged himself and others in the most difficult circumstances to utilize dialogue as a way of building greater understanding between people. Nabil has continued to be engaged in dialogue opportunities for reconciliation between conflicting traditions and cultures.

Building Peace in the Middle of Crisis and War is Possible

There are three foundational principles that must exist for peace to have a chance in our world and communities.

First, it is critical that we humanize one to the other. Dehumanizing the other always brings conflict and strife and derails any path to peace.

Second, each side needs to understand the pain and fear of the other. They do not have to agree but they must understand.

Third, practice peacebuilding conduct based on the mantra of **LISTEN - THINK - ACT**. This practice requires us to think critically rather than jump to conclusions or buy into stereotypes, misinformation and "fake news". It requires us to be attentive, reflective and act from a space of knowledge and certainty.

Building peace is not easy. I can share from personal experience; utilizing these principles needs patience and perseverance. It needs a realistic mind and a hopeful heart.

I just spent the past few weeks in a war zone and experienced the hard work of peacebuilding in action. Through storytelling and cooperative learning, community peacebuilders were working within their communities to mitigate conflict. I also witnessed them bringing people from opposing sides of the conflict together. They sat and expressed their feelings and their anxieties and started to explore possible paths to healing and building trust.

Leaders and activists came together for a restoration process where opposing sides were asked to share the story of the "other" as they heard it from individuals from the other side. This was very transformative and had a serious constructive impact on these leaders.

I saw these activities as true rays of hope. Peace is possible when we put in the work.

Mehmet Ateş - Türkiye

Mehmet Ateş is the coordinator of Servas Peace Schools in Ekinci-Aydi, Antakya-Hatay, Türkiye, not far from the border with Syria.   www.servas.org/peace-schools

Peace: Embracing and Learning from Diversity
The Servas Peace School

When international volunteers share their skills, knowledge and cultures with local children, families and each other, feelings of friendship and connection rise. Friendship and sharing between cultures bring peace, as it is more difficult to consider the idea of being in conflict with another culture or country when we are friends.

During the worst time of the war in Syria and after the devastating earthquake in Turkey in 2023, Servas Peace School volunteers struggled to help people reach the school, but we managed, and we came together. This feeling of solidarity that is created at these times creates peace. All in all, bringing people of the world together brings peace to the Earth.

Embracing more than 100 countries, Servas provides a network for its members to make contact, to build friendships and to broaden our understanding of the world. By connecting as hosts, travelers, or supporters, online or in person, we promote peace and tolerance, while encouraging environmentally sustainable meetings and lifestyles with less ecological impact.

The Servas Peace School is about sharing life practices and cultures. It aims to bring the knowledge and cultural riches of the world into our village in Turkey and build feelings of peace in children and local people. It introduces the multicultural background and peace experience of the city of Antakia with the world.

When people from different cultural backgrounds, from different parts of the world come to our village and stay with local families, a feeling of peace rises in the hearts and minds of visitors and hosts.

Yusuf (12), a student at the Peace School; "This place is not like a school at all. No one gets angry with us. There is no homework. It's like we are always on a break. We play games, learn languages, and learn about different countries and the people from Servas who come."

When we make the borders meaningless by bringing people of the world together, peace will grow and flourish naturally.

Suheir Freitekh - Palestine

Suheir Freitekh has a master's degree in Peace and Conflict Resolution from Haifa University and a second master's degree in International Studies from Birzeit University. Her dedication to learning about building peace in a war-torn land has continued over the last 20 years even though the Israeli occupation has become more encompassing and tightened over the years. She has worked with International NGOs and volunteered with local NGOs such as Palestine Israel Journal PIJ. She is a former and retired employee in Palestine Authority where she served as International Director in Nablus Governorate. Suheir is a Rotary Peace Fellow.

A Life Shaped by Conflict: A Journey of Search for Peace

I was born under the shadow of occupation, in a land where the sounds of war were woven into the fabric of everyday life. From the moment I took my first breath, the world around me was defined by conflict, and the notion of peace felt like a distant dream. My childhood was marked by uncertainty—daily struggles for survival, the constant threat of violence, and a growing understanding that safety was never guaranteed.

As I grew older, the weight of my surroundings became more apparent. Yet, despite the confusion, I found strength in the unspoken bonds of family and community. But surviving wasn't enough. I began to realize that to truly break the cycle of violence, I needed to seek something deeper—something more than just the absence of war. I came to understand that peace is not merely the cessation of conflict; it is the presence of justice, opportunity, and shared humanity.

This realization became the driving force of my life. I sought to learn more about peace, not just as an ideal, but as a practical, achievable goal. My commitment to fostering peace led me to get involved with Rotary peace activities, where I deepened my understanding of peace as a multifaceted concept—one that goes beyond the cessation of violence and encompasses social, economic, and cultural reconciliation.

But my desire to make a tangible impact didn't stop there. I co-founded an NGO called *Ufoq (Horizon)* because I wanted to offer my community a chance to build peace from the ground up. *Ufoq* was created to provide a platform for individuals to understand and experience peace, not as a distant dream, but as a living, breathing reality. Through educational programs, community dialogue, and advocacy, *Ufoq* works to equip individuals with the tools they need to break the cycle of violence and build a more just, peaceful society.

My involvement with *Ufoq* and Rotary has given me the opportunity to actively contribute to peacebuilding efforts, working alongside others who share the same vision for a world where peace is not

.

just the absence of conflict, but the active creation of understanding, opportunity, and respect.

Looking back on my journey—from surviving conflict to co-founding an organization dedicated to peace—I remain deeply committed to this cause. The experiences of my past have not only shaped who I am but have reinforced my belief in the power of peace to transform lives and communities.

Olena Zinenko - Ukraine

In **Olena Zinenko's** words: "I was born in Kharkiv, Ukraine, on September 28th, 1975. In middle school, I chose humanitarian studies. I was interested in journalism and became a culture activist, media practitioner, and media researcher. I graduated from Kharkiv State University as a philologist, worked as an editor on TV, a reporter in the press, a creative producer at an event agency, and a civil society consultant with Ukrainian NGOs. On the 24th of February 2022, I left my home city, Kharkiv, with my two daughters. We moved to the western part of Ukraine, to Lviv, and then to Krakow, Poland, and Frankfurt (Oder), Germany. On the road, I provided lectures online to my students at V.N.Karazin Kharkiv National University and Kharkiv State Academy of Culture. I defended my PhD at Jagiellonian University on the 23rd of February 2024. I wrote a book, " *Voices On the Road,*" about Ukrainian women who moved due to the Russian full-scale invasion of Ukraine."

Peacebuilding: Maintaining Connection

For humanity to find a way to peace for our world, our communities, and our societies we must first agree on what we understand by "peace". This concept is multifaceted, widely used and mostly corrupted in the world. I grew up in the USSR, when the slogans "We are for Peace!" were on every fence - literally. What did Soviet "peace" mean? It meant authoritarian pressure on citizens to support the state's aggressive global policy. This violent "peace" is still being promoted by Russian propaganda in Ukraine and around the world.

What does peace mean to me now? After Ukraine gained independence in 1991, we tried to avoid using Soviet slogans. We were against war. Year by year, Ukraine was giving up weapons, and the military complex was being destroyed.

When the war came in 2014 to the Donetsk and Luhansk regions, which neighbour my Kharkiv region, I joined the projects of civil society organisations. I met internally displaced people and conducted creative classes for children. That's when I started to understand what the destruction of peace is. One boy could not draw peace at all, he only drew war and snipers.

When the war came to my home in 2022 - I heard it in the distant explosions and saw it in the gun emplacements on the horizon of dawn - I left my home and took my peace with me. My peace was complemented by the stories of the women I met with at the

PeaceWomen Across the Globe roundtables.

They told me that peace is when you are safe when there is no war, when you are close to your loved ones when you are at home.

My opinion is that we should agree on the understanding of peace, agree on what it is. Having found a definition of peace, we need to think about what needs to be done to make it happen as we agreed.

I live in a hybrid reality - both online and offline. When I am not at home, not in Ukraine, I am mostly online. When I am at home, or when I visit Lviv, Kyiv, or Kharkiv, I live more offline, grounding myself, communicating with those I knew before the war. Or sometimes I meet virtually with those I have established connections with online.

The first thing I can recommend is to stay in touch. We are scattered all over the world, and our connection, memories, knowledge of the peace as it was and as it should be, keeps us together.

The second important thing is to tell our stories - about what war is and what peace is. This allows us to reconcile the realities of those who have not lived through experiences similar to ours.

Third, it is important to create conditions for networking, sharing experiences, and disseminating information. I am currently working on a project in which we aim to establish a connection between those women who stayed in Ukraine and those who went abroad to create joint peacebuilding projects in Ukraine.

It will be a dream come true.

Roslyn George - Trinidad and Tobago

Roslyn George has been the President of the Cashew Gardens Community Council in Trinidad and Tobago since 2006. During this time she has spearheaded all community activities and she has represented her community at the United Nations Commission for the Status of Women.

Coming Together for Understanding

Like the rest of the world, Trinidad and Tobago has been experiencing an unusual amount of violence and crime in reaction to domestic situations. This seems to be a time where persons are no longer willing to have dialogue, but conflict is settled with guns and knives and other weapons and, in many cases, death.

We have experienced the deterioration of our own moral fabric, and it seems to be irreparable.

There was a time when people respected and embraced each other's differences, a young person would address an elder person respectfully as aunty or uncle even if they were not related by blood and everyone had a deep regard for a higher power. Children were raised with tolerance, worship and meditation, and it did not matter what beliefs a persons ascribed to, the basic tenets were the same that one should 'love your neighbor as yourself'.

As a multicultural, multi-religious, and multiethnic society, our people have always practiced tolerance for everyone and celebrated our unique offerings.

Just as the world is faced with numerous challenges - conflicts, violence, and the pursuit of limited resources that threaten the very fabric of peace - so too are the hearts and minds of people who are led to believe that the only way to solve conflict is with violence and force.

Though we recognize that the journey towards peace is not an easy one, as global citizens who are just passing through, we need to get back to that place where human life has value, where people's opinion matter, where we see each other as a fellow man who has our own contribution to make to the world, and where our respect and adoration for a higher power would influence our decisions when conflict arise.

We must continue to work towards a peaceful world as we long for harmony, understanding, and coexistence.

Vidal Campos Magno - Timor L'Este

Vidal Campos Magno is a Rotary Peace Fellow and a Peace Jam alumnus. He is a speaker for Conflict Resolution and Mediation with RYLA – Leadership Training and a teacher trainer. He works with the NGO Ba Futuru and as Ba Futures' National Program Manager, leads Ba Futuru's diverse range of peacebuilding programs. Ba Futuru / For the Future is a leading Timorese not-for-profit organization, specializing in peacebuilding, gender empowerment, child protection education, teaching approaches and conflict transformation. www.bafuturu.org

Bringing Peace and Hope to A New Country

I became a peacebuilder because, in 1999, Timor L'Este held a popular referendum and, as a result, separated from Indonesia, becoming the youngest country in the world. This move toward independence sparked interstate and intrastate conflict and over time Timor L'Este became a post-conflict country.

In the face of the conflict, I chose to be a peacebuilder and, in doing so, provided training workshops with the goal of developing peacebuilding skills to those in all targeted groups in the conflict. These workshops were designed to help find a path to resolve and mitigate conflict in our communities.

At the same time, I have been committed to work that specifically protects women and children as they are the most vulnerable groups in conflict and most likely to become the victims. Advocating for women and girls is key to building sustainable peace in our country.

Targeted and skilled peacebuilding, based in the Pillars of Positive Peace, is an important instrument to ensure that all people feel safe in their own community.

Maintaining peace and unity is essential for providing opportunities for improved economic and social development for all people, especially in a young country such as Timor L'Este.

This world needs peace in order for people to survive and thrive. This is true for all facing conflict and crises including wars, pollution, natural disasters and more.

When peace and harmony are maintained, it provides peaceful options for those who are faced with potential conflict and wish to disengage, or not engage, in disruptive or conflict-based activities, such as were present in Timor L'Este.

Aleksandra Minkiewicz - Myanmar

Aleksandra Minkiewicz has over two decades of professional experience in communications and international development work, including over 10 years of working experience on media development, human rights and educational programmes in conflict-affected countries with limited civic space like Myanmar, South Sudan and Afghanistan. As a Director of the Yangon Film School (YFS) she was responsible for the development of a more inclusive and diverse media sector by training young multi-ethnic Burmese filmmakers and producing documentary films and other media formats about the situation of human rights in Myanmar. Aleksandra oversaw the design and implementation of the outreach and engagement strategy supporting disadvantaged communities and civil society organizations, by advocating for the free flow of information and increased cooperation between CSOs and media. She was particularly focused on the 'Women & Peace' project promoting gender mainstreaming by training women in leadership roles in the media, in particular illuminating the role of women in the peace process.

Media and the Role of Women and Youth in Everyday Peace

The path to global peace requires inclusive efforts that engage youth, women, and diverse voices within society. In 2017 Nobel Prize Laureate, Daw Aung San Suu Kyi, emphasised the importance of involving all citizens of Myanmar in the peace process and highlighted the crucial roles of women and youth.

Women bring unique perspectives to peacebuilding, playing vital roles in re-establishing social fabric after conflict. Their inclusion significantly increases the chances of lasting peace, yet they remain underrepresented in peace and security narratives in the media.

Myanmar's transition from six decades of authoritarian rule to democracy faces significant challenges, including military control, deep-seated ethnic and religious divisions, and media censorship.

Initiatives such as Yangon Film School (YFS) have been instrumental in promoting freedom of expression and empowering a generation of multi-ethnic young media workers. By creating films that highlight human rights issues and promote diversity, filmmakers support an inclusive peace process.

The media - the "fourth estate" of democracy - plays a pivotal role in shaping public discourse and promoting peace. To create an independent and diverse media, it is essential to train skilled filmmakers, men and women, coming from all walks of life, who can promote inter-ethnic and inter-cultural dialogue, and foster social cohesion. Robust media education and freedom of speech are critical for helping the public develop informed opinions.

Since Myanmar's military deposed the democratically elected government in 2021, the operating environment for media has deteriorated dramatically.

Professional media workers and filmmakers are in hiding or imprisoned. Many changed their profession or emigrated to other countries seeking stable income. This created a gap in the media and filmmaking industry that will take a long time to rebuild. At this crucial point in Myanmar's history, continuous efforts to strengthen film as means of promoting diversity, democratisation and peace must not be hindered by funding cuts or a focus on humanitarian aid.

International support and advocacy for equitable participation of multi-ethnic representation of youth and women in the peacebuilding and reconciliation process is critical. If half the population is excluded, peace will be impossible to achieve. Sharing women's and young people's stories with a wider audience will bring a better understanding of their contribution to building sustainable peace.

Audio-visual tools support efforts of conflict mitigation by breaking down fears and anxieties about 'the other', giving a voice to marginalised and vulnerable groups, and by reaching out to remote communities with screenings and discussions. Film, especially documentary, serves everyone's longing for truth and encourages audiences to reflect on actions and attitudes.

The need for strong, humane films is more urgent than ever in Myanmar, where misinformation and hate speech escalate tensions. Films that encourage reflection and dialogue help bridge divides and foster reconciliation in a country still grappling with the legacy of conflict.

Daniel Carlsen Pol - Bolivia

Daniel Carlsen Pol has a Masters in Corporate and Business Law with a specialty in Corporate Social Responsibility from the Universidad Andina Simón Bolívar and diplomas in Higher Education, Human Rights to Food, and Corporate Social Responsibility. He currently teaches at the undergraduate and postgraduate level and is the President and General Director of the Hagamos el Cambio Foundation and Country Director of the International Youth Society, and Member of the Professional Community of Empresability/ Ibero-American Movement of Social Responsibility and of World Beyond War, Bolivia Chapter.

Change Our World Through Education

We are living in a world where the business of chaos, death, and suffering are the most lucrative businesses; where the perfect ingredients for survival seem to be being mean, aggressive, and taking advantage of others, without caring for the impact of these actions on others and on our communities.

In countries like Bolivia, which is a very conflicted and unstable country, the result of this business of aggression and greed is that now, in comparison to the 1990's, feeding a family has become extremely expensive, making it insufficient to have one family income. Two adults in a family must work to create sufficient income. As a result, children don't receive the same level of support and education from their parents as they used to. This includes children not having the opportunity to

learn about values and ethics from spending time with their parents.

At the same time, schools and universities have adopted new perspectives, viewing their students as clients who are promoted without having had the opportunity to learn. The quality of education and the level of students' achievement have significantly decreased in Bolivia, and the content of what they are learning has not changed in 50 or 60 years.

So, in my humble opinion, I believe that what needs to happen for humanity to find a way to peace for our world, our communities and our societies are the following actions:

Modify the curriculum in educational institutions by including subjects such as care for the environment; how to cook, home economics, and animal protection, as well as teaching skills such as respect, teamwork and collaboration.

Focus on the importance of growing the "three muscles": mind, heart and hands. This means that education must not only be about learning information, (mind) but also, learning with compassion, empathy and understanding, about the needs and issues facing the community (heart) and, lastly, but also extremely important, learning to develop and implement solutions for the specific situation in the community based on this understanding (hand).

Teach the fundamentals of building a culture of peace: Starting an educational process with children from the age of six that is based on the principles of a culture of peace will create a generation of socially responsible changemakers. Children who are taught leadership, emotional intelligence, active listening, negotiations, creation and execution of projects will become teenagers and future professionals with a high level of social awareness and responsibility, and our future peacebuilders.

As Nelson Mandela said, "The most important weapon to change the world is education."

Chris Batchilder - Canada

Chris Batchilder dedicated over three decades of his life to serving in the Canadian Armed Forces as a Signals Intelligence Specialist. Throughout his service, Chris actively participated in numerous deployments across the globe including Bosnia, Afghanistan, Kuwait, and Iraq. In addition to these international missions, Chris also participated in critical domestic operations across Canada, including the provision of military assistance during flood and ice storm emergencies. As well as postings in Canada, he has participated in exchange postings, working with both the US Army and US Navy.

A Soldier's Perspective on Peacebuilding

As a 30-year Canadian Armed Forces Veteran I believe that promoting peace in the world requires bravery and the commitment to create long-lasting stability and harmony. From my perspective as a Canadian soldier, achieving peace involves a mix of military discipline and a strong focus on diplomacy, education, economic stability, and empathy. By emphasizing these areas, soldiers can help create a more peaceful and just world.

Canadian soldiers know how important it is to build strong relationships with other countries. Canada's history of peacebuilding demonstrates that communication and teamwork can help avoid conflicts and resolve issues peacefully. Working with and keeping in touch with other countries and organizations like the United Nations is crucial for global safety.

Education is also very important for building peace. Soldiers often take part in training programs in conflict areas to help local communities maintain peace and security. By supporting education that fosters critical thinking, tolerance, and human rights, they help shape a future where people value peace.

Soldiers see firsthand how poverty can lead to unrest and how economic stability can contribute to peacebuilding. In peacekeeping missions, forces can support projects that encourage economic growth and self-reliance in local communities and by helping people access resources and opportunities, they work to reduce the causes of violence.

Through empathy and understanding Canadian soldiers learn to appreciate different cultures and viewpoints in their diverse work environments. This experience highlights the need for open dialogue and building trust. By engaging with communities and supporting local initiatives, soldiers help create respect and reduce conflict among different groups.

Additionally, soldiers understand the importance of involving peacebuilders, such as women, youth, and marginalized communities, who often provide unique insights for peace efforts. By supporting their participation and amplifying their voices, soldiers help create more effective and lasting peace solutions.

It is these areas that give a soldier a unique perspective into promoting peace in the world. If more people were able to see the world from this perspective, I believe that world peace could be realized.

Jamal Saeed - Syria and Canada

Jamal Saeed spent twelve years as a prisoner of conscience in Syria before being invited to Canada in 2016. He continues to raise awareness about Syria's humanitarian crisis through his work as an activist, editor, visual artist, and author. He lives in Kingston, Ontario.

On the Border

On the Lebanese side of the border between Syria and Lebanon, I stood with my family and about two hundred other Syrians under the June sun waiting for our turn to have our papers stamped. I was looking at the children in front of a building whose sign read *Lebanese General Directorate of Security*.

Everyone wanted to protect their children and themselves from the death caused by the shells, bullets, explosive barrels dropped by helicopters and knives carried by extremist militias to slaughter people.

It occurred to me that we, who do not have weapons and do not want to have weapons, number more than twenty-three million, out of 24 million Syrians, and yet we are subject to about one million people who carry weapons. And here we are being displaced from our homes, even from our country. And here on the border, we stand like beggars to obtain an entry visa to a neighboring country.

I saw lizards, butterflies, flies and birds crossing the border without documents, a tree extending its branches to cross the border without anyone's permission, and the scent of a rose crossing the border and throwing its perfume into the air as if it were writing the biography of its short life, not caring about the border police, their uniforms and their individual weapons.

It occurred to me that day that the Earth could be a beautiful homeland for humans when it is free of wars and weapons, and when it is free of borders as well.

Then no one will force me to leave my home, and I will choose where I will live and how I will roam the Earth, to plant what my soul carries of love and songs for the Earth inhabited by peace, freedom and justice.

I felt that I have friends everywhere all over the world, they have pure and warm souls, but I haven't met them all yet.

Chapter Six: Discovering Alternatives

"To replace the old paradigm of war with a new paradigm of waging peace, we must be pioneers who can push the boundaries of human understanding. We must be doctors who can cure the virus of violence. We must be soldiers of peace who can do more than preach to the choir. And we must be artists who will make the world our masterpiece."

- Paul Chappell *(Peace activist, former soldier, 1980 – present, USA)*

In the last chapter, Gary Mason recommends that people challenge their thinking by asking "maybe, just maybe", thereby identifying and considering new possibilities, ideas and solutions that are not readily apparent to them. Similarly, the contributors to this chapter encourage us to think more broadly and challenge ourselves, and especially the peacebuilding community, to consider alternatives and openly, without prejudice, discuss research and technology that may enhance established peacebuilding practices, or maybe, just maybe, provide new directions.

These contributors tackle the questions: Are there new ways, new tools, or new ideas that we can apply to our peacebuilding work? What happens when we reach out to people and build connections through music or through sport? What does AI offer to us? What can we explore with quantum physics? What can we learn from other sectors about practicing peace effectively and ethically? What would happen if we re-structure our systems to support a peaceful future? And how does changing our language change our actions?

We know that change is the most predictable aspect of human nature and our human history. When we welcome new ideas, act and question with curiosity and explore unfamiliar ways of understanding, we may be better able to direct the change toward peace rather than conflict.

"For things to reveal themselves to us, we need to be ready to abandon our views about them."
- Thich Nhat Hanh

Thania Paffenholz - Kenya

Thania Paffenholz is the founder of the Association for Inclusive Peace (previously the Inclusive Peace and Transition Initiative) and Senior Fellow of the Centre for Conflict, Development and Peacebuilding, Graduate Institute of International and Development Studies, Geneva. She is internationally renowned for her work on and in support of peace and political transition processes, focusing on mediation, negotiations, peacebuilding and National Dialogues, process design, inclusion, and participation, as well as the conditions under which peace processes produce sustainable outcomes. Thania holds a PhD in International Relations with focus on mediation and peacebuilding, has published widely, and is the founder of Inclusive Peace.

www.inclusivepeace.org

Setting Change in Motion: Lessons Learned from 30 Years of Building Peace

For the past 30 years, I have facilitated peace processes in more than 25 countries and have been writing and speaking about the lessons learned globally. It is a humbling journey, focusing on inspiring local activists to recognize the power they hold to initiate change, working with armed groups and governments to find pathways out of war, and navigating the many resistances to change. I also engage with international actors, striving to help them support, rather than inadvertently block, the changes necessary for peace.

Peacebuilding is a perpetual process. It is the ongoing renegotiation of the social and political contract within societies. A central question is: who participates in these conversations, and what are the power

dynamics involved? Too often, only the "guys with the guns" are included in peace talks, while the rest of the population is excluded. In recent years, there has been a push for broader inclusion of non-armed political and societal groups, but these efforts often feel cosmetic. For example, in Syria, Libya, and Afghanistan, attempts at inclusion were superficial and largely symbolic. Genuine inclusion occurs when excluded groups make a compelling case for their involvement, as in the Colombian peace process between the government and the FARC where mass mobilization by excluded actors drove their participation.

The question remains: what is inclusion for? Nepal offers a compelling example. During the National Dialogue negotiations, a quota system was implemented to ensure representation for underprivileged ethnic and societal groups, including women and lower castes. After the negotiation process, this quota system evolved into affirmative action, enabling these groups to become integral participants in political and societal decision-making processes.

Societies are constantly evolving, and peace processes represent critical junctures where change becomes more likely. Yet, the planning and implementation of peace processes is transforming as the world undergoes profound changes. The post-1990s world order, dominated by a liberal peace and economic model is ending. From Afghanistan to Iraq to Somalia, peace did not become a reality for most people; instead, power and resources were simply redistributed among a select few.

Now, we are witnessing the rise of new powers in the so-called Global South and the Gulf states, bringing different approaches to ending wars. The old system has yet to relinquish its grip, while the emerging new order remains unsettled.

Globally, we find ourselves in a period of transition, moving from the old to the new. This emerging order will not be a binary opposite of the old but rather a diverse and heterogeneous landscape.

Achieving peace requires far more than expertise. Peacebuilding is an art—the art of transforming the impossible into the possible while remaining mindful of the ultimate destination. It extends beyond the mere cessation of armed conflict. True peacebuilding is about setting change in motion to create inclusive societies that remain dynamic and adaptable. This journey also requires a deeper recognition of our relationship with nature. Peacebuilding is holistic and encompasses not only peace within societies but also peace within ourselves. The key is not to give up but to continue acting, supporting, connecting, and inspiring and being inspired from the hearts and minds. In this harmony lies the power to create lasting change and to keep the journey of peacebuilding alive and meaningful.

Spencer Leung - Thailand

In 2011, Hong Kong native **Spencer Leung** moved to Thailand to launch the organic operation of a Thai agricultural seed company. He believed that demand for organic food would continue to expand, but he didn't simply want to make money. He wanted to do something good. Recognizing that creating economic stability for small farmers will promote peace, he launched Go Organics, which helps farmers who cultivate less than 2 hectares (about 5 acres) of crops to improve their productivity and sustainability. Spencer is a Rotary Peace Fellow and the Founder of GO Organics Peace International.

Promoting the Use of Permaculture Ethics for Peacebuilding

The world is a mess. In most Western mainstream media, we hear daily about the atrocities from the fighting in Ukraine and the suffering of the Palestinians in Gaza and the Middle East.

Imperialism, geopolitics, nationalism, greed, and self-interest are usually to blame for these sufferings. With this mindset, one can be passive in action, thinking that there can be nothing an ordinary citizen like oneself can do to rectify these physical acts of violence.

While an authoritative, top-down approach may temporarily halt harmful physical violence, lasting peacebuilding can only be achieved at the community grassroots level through committed and gradual individual actions. With the appropriate mindset, everyone can play a vital role.

During peace studies, we talk about inner peace, social peace, and environmental peace as if these classifications of peace are distinct at different levels, from self-care to people care to caring for our ecosystem and planet.

Although peace activists, perhaps for self-care purposes, must think about achieving inner peace first before addressing the needs of others, as an environmentalist, permaculturalist, and Rotary Peace Fellow, I argue that unless we know where we are on this land, we shall not know ourselves, let alone bring peace within our inner-self and others.

Although global climate change may be natural, human activities have exacerbated it since the Industrial Revolution. Increased environmental and climate displacement of people caused by erratic

146

climate patterns and ecological disasters have further strained the turbulent world.

By 2050, the world population will reach nearly 10 billion, almost tenfold compared to the population during the Industrial Revolution. When the earth's natural resources are finite, each person will have fewer resources in their possession. Humans' built-in self-protection mechanism will kick in, fighting for resources for self-preservation, creating more conflicts in addition to the unpredictable climates.

Paul Hawken states, "What people want in their place is universal: security, the ability to support their families, educational opportunities, nutritious and affordable food, clean water, sanitation, and access to health care," and a Native American rightly said to Hawken, "The way we harm the earth affects all people, and how we treat one another is reflected in how we treat the earth." [12]

Since the earth's problems are everyone's problems, and organisms within our ecosystem, including humans, are intertwined, to take action in building peace, what we can do is to cross-learn, practice, and promote the Three Ethics of Permaculture: Earth Care, People Care, and Fair Share and have these ethics act as a checklist in everyone's daily life.

Ultimately, how can we bring peace to ourselves and others if we cannot learn to share with others and bring peace to our planet?

---

[12] Hawkens, Paul. *Blessed Unrest.* (2008) Penguin Books

Anne Hebert - Australia

Anne Herbert is a semi-retired educator and change-maker based in Australia who now devotes most of her time to the Alternatives to Violence Project, Friends Peace Teams, and other peacebuilding activities including gardening, bushwalking, and camping.

www.avp.international   www.friendspeaceteams.org

Investing in Peace

"The intractable challenges facing us—from the climate crisis to white supremacy to the horror of conventional and nuclear war—will not be resolved using the timeworn scripts of avoidance, aversion, accommodation, or attack. What's needed more than ever is the engine of nonviolent change, a force for waging conflict creatively and effectively." — Ken Butigan

In the 21st century, even though we know that an eye for an eye can lead to everyone becoming blind, we can seem inescapably embroiled in ways of processing conflicts that depend on violence. At least, a common assumption seems to be that if we don't get what we want other ways, using violent means will be reasonable.

Imagine if we had invested as much time, energy, and resources in pursuing non-military, non-violent, just solutions. Where might we be now?

Certainly, most of us would have many more skills in non-violent negotiation and a larger toolkit (that does not include the development and deployment of military solutions) to apply when conflict emerges. A peace-building-industrial complex rather than a military-industrial complex?

Would we have less conflict? Not necessarily, but we would process it very differently. I do not think that finding a way to peace means we will avoid conflict. Conflict will always arise due to tensions between differences in life and interests. As many authors have elaborated, difference, diversity and conflicts can be the source of creativity, the driver for trying all sorts of possible ways forward.

How can we seek, identify, and hold onto the sources of creativity in conflict, and use that energy to pursue constructive, power-sharing ways forward?

This big question will never have a single answer, so we continuously draw on established understandings and prior experiences to apply and adjust in the present.

Importantly we need to remain fit and flexible, to be ready to try and test different ways, adapting to the demands of the specific moment.

Fitness and flexibility to creatively process conflicts with peaceful intent is possible. Knowledge, skills, and systems can be developed through research, education and practice, nurtured by strong global institutions, government commitments at multiple levels, in workplaces, civil society organisations, and households, and in community activities.

To become the norm, the prioritisation of peaceful and just options needs to be institutionalised at all levels of our society.

Serious financial investment and recognition of the urgency to do the work are required to invent new ways to create, practise, and sustain peace and justice. This is not protest or only 'voluntary' activity for 'alternative' people. This is serious, challenging hard work that requires quite as much - or more - money and infrastructure than military and related violent options. Let this work become mainstream, more common than building, trading, and deploying arms. Let's redirect economic and creative resources into a wide variety of efforts for the germination, gestation, resilience and life cycle of building peace and justice without violence. Let's lobby corporations, governments, and influencers everywhere to invest in peacebuilding.

Let's change the assumption that resorting to violence is reasonable, and make the assumption that we continuously seek peaceful, just resolutions.

Pamela Huerta - Mexico

Pamela Huerta is an international development professional with over ten years of work experience including program design, management and evaluation. She has held positions at the government, corporate and INGO sectors, and has broad multicultural experience studying and working in Latin America, Europe and Southeast Asia. She has provided design, monitoring and evaluation (DME) services to the U.S. State Department, the Bureau of International Narcotics and Law Enforcement Affairs/ Western Hemisphere Programs (INL/WHP), and the USAID and the IADB, among other organizations. She also had the opportunity to open her scope of expertise, engaging in projects in Mexico and Honduras. Pamela was part of the team leading the Crime and Violence Prevention Program at the Ministry of the Interior in Mexico.

Investing in Peace through Design, Monitoring, Evaluation and Learning

There are countless things needed to build and sustain peace. During the last years, I have worked with different organisations to improve their design, monitoring and evaluation systems. From this side, I believe there is still a lot of work to be done, and I'd like to put forward some basic ideas that I consider vital to adopt in any peacebuilding activity.

First, evidence shows that multi-stakeholder involvement has an impact in increasing the likelihood of sustained peace. In this sense, participatory methods should be encouraged throughout all phases and, particularly in the design stage, we need to ensure the participation of all relevant stakeholders, especially those most vulnerable.

Community-led initiatives through participatory methods are the key to determining what peace is and creating a common vision of what are we looking for and the steps to achieve it. It is key to identify both resilience and vulnerability components – local capacities, social safety nets, and risks. And lastly, participatory methods should also be utilized to support learning and adaptive management of programs throughout the implementation.

Secondly, peace does not happen overnight. We must acknowledge peace as a process, where incorporating learning through robust monitoring is crucial.

While most donors require programs with an M&E component, there is still room to make programs flexible enough and to allow them to incorporate learning loops throughout the implementation. This is especially important in crises, where some projects may need to shift rapidly according to the context and possibilities. Organisations also struggle when trying to go from having data to actually using it. Program designs must allow iterations to incorporate learning and use both qualitative and quantitative data to inform decision-making processes.

And finally, programs need to generate evidence and knowledge through evaluation. There have been more attempts to conduct evaluations in the peace and development sectors, but there are still a lot of gaps on how programs contribute to change, what the expected and unexpected results are, what works under which circumstances, and what does not work and why. Programs must encourage evaluations to cover these knowledge gaps. In the mid and long terms, this would help practitioners to build robust theories of change, implement evidence-based programming, and in the end, contribute to sustained peace. Finally, the learning process also helps us to reflect on what we achieve, what we did not, and how to move forward.

Peace is very complex and sometimes a bit fuzzy, but applying robust design, monitoring, evaluation and learning tools may contribute to having better and more sustained results.

Diego Carneiro - Brazil/Ecuador

Diego Carneiro was born in Belém, in the Amazon region of Brazil. Diego moved to Quito, Ecuador in 2016, where he has been pursuing a dual career as conductor of the Orquesta Joven del Ecuador (Youth Orchestra of Ecuador) and as a concert cellist. In recent years, the Orquesta Joven del Ecuador has become a musical home for refugees from Venezuela and other South American countries, allowing them to continue the music education that was begun in their home countries. Diego established AmazonArt, a foundation with the mission of "changing lives through music." AmazonArt promotes innovative concerts in developing countries, using music to foster cultural exchange between nations. He is a Rotary Peace Fellow.

www.amazonarts.org.

Orchestrating Peace, a Symphony of Love

Peace must be cultivated, nurtured from the grassroots to a global scale. It starts with embracing diversity, understanding one another, and learning the value of service. My journey as a musician and advocate for harmony has revealed how music transcends barriers, creating unity and solace even in the most challenging circumstances.

Music is more than an art form—it is a universal language and bridge. Since I was 12 years old, I have been not only performing in mainstream festivals and halls but also in refugee camps, hospitals, impoverished neighborhoods and prisons where individuals face immense physical and emotional hardships. In these places music becomes a source of strength, elevating spirits, fostering well-being, and

forming a sense of community. It soothes aggression, transforms conflict zones, and merges cultural differences. When music touches a soul, it has the potential to transform lives.

My first public performance was my first encounter with the transformative power of music. As a child, performing for elderly residents in a care home, I saw how music brought relief and joy to those listening. A few months later my first official concert took place at the Teatro da Paz (Peace Theater) in Belém, Brazil. That name, "Peace", has resonated throughout my career, shaping my mission and identity.

Today, I create an emotional performance experience rather than mere concerts. I have collaborated with communities impacted by hunger, illness, and displacement, using music as a means to restore dignity, hope, and connection. These encounters have taught me that peace begins with truly listening—not just to melodies, but to the stories, challenges, and dreams of others.

I view music as a potent instrument for fostering peace. It energizes younger generations, inspires compassion, and nurtures understanding. It unites diverse cultures, encouraging collaboration and mutual respect. I have witnessed the profound impact music has on communities, dismantling barriers and building enduring connections.

This vision has guided the creation of Amazon Arts, Friends of Music in the Americas, and Orchestrating Peace. Each initiative flows from the same source—a commitment to leveraging music for a more harmonious world. Our causes address environmental, indigenous causes, education, cultural exchange, refugees, hunger health, for example, and the creation of Youth orchestras and a music school. I dream of building several peace theaters in different countries!

As an artist, I believe we carry a profound responsibility: to uplift humanity. Music teaches us to exist "in harmony", both literally and metaphorically. It emphasizes the importance of cooperation, the strength of empathy, and the beauty of shared connection.

Peace is like a symphony and each of us plays a vital role. Together, we can compose a melody that resonates across borders, guiding us toward a more equitable and compassionate future.

Elaine Pratley - Australia

Elaine Pratley is a lawyer, social entrepreneur, and peace advocate living and working in Melbourne, Australia. She holds a PhD in Peace Studies and Conflict Resolution from the University of Melbourne. She is associated with the Monash Global Peace and Security (GPS) Centre and is the founder of Peace Inc. and Peace Kitchen. She is a Rotary Peace Fellow.

Quantum Physics and Peacebuilding: Surprising Connections

Quantum physics offers unique perspectives into peacebuilding. Traditionally, peace principles are often discussed in socio-political terms, but quantum physics provides a scientific language to complement these frameworks.

Both quantum physics and conflict transformation view the world as dynamic and changeable. For example, quantum physics sees matter as simultaneously moving waves and static particles (the 'wave-particle duality'). The material world is paradoxically fixed and constantly becoming. Similarly, conflict transformation acknowledges that peace and conflict coexist and transform each other. These perspectives contrast with rigid dualistic views, emphasizing a spectrum of evolving possibilities.

Both disciplines also recognize the interconnectedness and agency of the world. A gun, though hanging rigidly on a wall, can trigger a range of emotions and responses. As part of an ecosystem of things and ideas, it 'causes' reactions even without human intervention. Likewise, conflict transformation highlights the interconnectedness of the human world, where individual flourishing is paradoxically a collective effort. For the inhabitants of Tuvalu to survive, people worldwide must take climate action.

These shared perspectives offer hope. Both disciplines see potential in 'the void' (the absence of particulate matter) and in death, emphasizing that nothing is fixed but always evolving and holding potential for growth. We are not stuck in a fixed state of being but always in the process of becoming.

While some may find it unexpected, these parallels between physics and peace work are significant and should not be surprising. Peace is an idea long pondered before Johan Galtung popularised 'positive peace'. Peacebuilding draws from ancient,

Indigenous, and Asian wisdoms, much like quantum entanglement resonates with ideas from ancient philosophers across cultures.

Science offers fresh opportunities for peacebuilding. Viewing peacebuilding through a scientific lens challenges traditional academic norms and gives credibility to marginalized perspectives. In essence, whether through scientific or traditional lenses, embracing ideas of change and interconnectedness is crucial for the future of peacebuilding.

Catherine Ali - Trinidad and Tobago

Catherine Ali is a conflict transformation professional and consultant in the change energy of gender empowerment and human development. Her background is in researching social problems and developing social policy concerning social, criminal, and restorative justice.

Discovering New Possibilities

In deep conflict, I was carried through unspeakable pain and held while the hole in my soul bled out. Effortlessly, my perspectives pivoted as solidarity, protection and fluidity provided peace conditions.

New dimensions of solidarity were received as my head poked through clouds into unimagined power, awaiting deployment. Empowerment (feminism), vibration frequencies (quantum energy), consciousness (spirit), insight (conflict resolution), describe discovering new ranges of possibilities.

Bubble-wrapped in protection, I breathed in conflict without vomiting bile. Insulation brought freedom to observe, chew, assimilate and integrate suffering to reconstitute meanings of past violent events. New interpretations generated different futures. Within abundance, trauma-bonds attenuated, dysregulation eased. When not defending low frequencies, letting go flows into higher dimensions of strength and peace. Fluidity distilled suffering, lotus-like, into fruit that I am free to distribute as I choose. Peace resonance consciously creates better futures from barbarity, by expanding into multi-dimensional frequencies that eliminate powerlessness, provide a basic social platform below which no one falls, advancing global well-being. Feminists evoke consciousness, scientists are discovering it, mystics dwell in it, peacebuilders sense its evolving.

A prayer found beside a child's body at Ravensbruck Death Camp, considers people of ill-will encountering (self) judgement.* From the suffering they caused, fruit borne from its absorption and distillation through fifth dimension human personhood, was redirected to restorative processes, pivoting realities.

I'm grateful for life's paradox; destructive experiences opened compassion gifts; gratitude eclipsed the powerlessness gestating violence. As systems crumble globally, conditions ripen for equitable inclusive quantum peace systems, as soon as we wish to discover and action them.

156

O Lord, remember, not only the men and women of good will, but also those of ill will. But do not remember all the suffering they have inflicted on us; remember the fruits we have borne, thanks to this suffering: our comradeship, our loyalty, our humility, our courage, our generosity, the greatness of heart which has grown out of all this, and when they come to judgement, let all the fruits we have borne be their forgiveness.

A prayer from a Jewish victim at Ravensbrück – St Thomas and St Bede". thomasandbede.com. Retrieved 2021-06-08.

Tom Woodhouse, Emeritus Professor University of Bradford UK; Visiting Professor Ramon Llul University Barcelona Spain; Institute for Economics and Peace International Advisory Council; Independent Football Ombudsman – Adviser on Football and Community, President Peace Studies FC, Academic Editor for Routledge Series on Peace and Conflict Resolution.

www.football4community.co.uk   www.golesporlapaz.org

Give Peace a Sporting Chance: Football, the SDGs and Peacebuilding

In June 2024 the Department of Peace Studies and International Development at the University of Bradford in the UK celebrated its 50th anniversary. Over these fifty years, and now as an Emeritus Professor, I have spent much of my professional life working in the fields of conflict resolution and peacebuilding.

In recent years I have become convinced that we need to reach out beyond our somewhat comfortable and constrained academic perspectives to develop new sources of creativity, renewal and innovation in our peacebuilding work.

For me, the perfect way to do this is to unite my two passions, (often not connected and even by some seen as polar opposites), that is a love of sport and peace. In this 'passion peace', I explain why I am excited by this potential to link sport, and especially football/soccer (the world game) with peacebuilding.

The 2030 Agenda for Sustainable Development, adopted by all United Nations members in 2015, identified 17 world Sustainable Development Goals (SDGs). They were created with the aim of achieving peace and prosperity for people and the planet.

When football engages with the UN Agenda 2030, a powerful energy is generated, capable of sending a new peace message with unparalleled power to connect the local with the global. There are many ways in which football clubs, with the resources and the unparalleled social capital they have in their communities, have an impact on local SDGs and peacebuilding activities.

The UN has declared that sport has special relevance, particularly in the realms of SDG 3 (healthy lives and well-being), SDG 4 (inclusive education and lifelong learning), SDG 5 (gender equality and empower all women and girls), SDG 11 (inclusive, safe, resilient and sustainable cities), SDG 16 (just, peaceful and inclusive societies) and SDG 17 (global partnership for sustainable development).

To take just one case study among many, the peace process in Colombia provides an excellent example of how this works in practice. In 2016 the Colombian President Juan Manuel Santos was awarded the Nobel Peace Prize for a peace deal signed with FARC rebels which ended the 52-year-old conflict. Santos used the national obsession with football ('the only thing that unites us') to reframe the dialogue about the conflict from one of nationalism to inclusivity. The peace agreement has held and is rightly cited as an outstanding example of sustainable post-conflict peacebuilding. In 2022 the United Nations launched Football for the Goals, a platform for the global football community to engage with the 17 Sustainable Development Goals.

Sport for development approaches is now used at the community level throughout Colombia. One such project is Goles por la Paz, based in the Olas Dos barrio in the city of Bucaramanga.

Formed in 2009, Goles por la Paz works with children and young people to enable them to play a part in the emergence of a culture of peace in their communities. With the support of the Institute for Economics and Peace, Goles por la Paz is currently developing a pioneering project to orientate its activities to support the SDGs, in a way that is relevant to the needs of the community, as defined by the young people.

At the same time, the IEP's eight-pillar model for cultivating positive peace is used to integrate the SDGs into a holistic model for community peacebuilding in post-conflict Colombia – a perfect example of the local-global connection, where local ownership drives global goals.

Frances Jeffries - USA

Frances Jeffries is a consultant to non-profit organizations focused on peace initiatives in developing countries. She completed a PhD in Counseling Psychology at Kent State University and has worked professionally in all types of educational settings, as well as in several community-based organizations. She has shared her home with nine children.

Peace for Our World. Humanity United for Peace

These phrases and themes recur in talks, media and countless other places. But, despite the words and, quite likely, the intent, we live in a world filled with traumatized individuals, conflicts within communities and nations, intercountry wars and the never-ending build-up of weapons and aggressive strategies.

For humanity to find a way to peace for our world, our communities, and our societies, we must first be willing to begin with where we stand at this moment. It may not be "perfect," but it is, in fact, all that we have. Transformation from conflict to peace will involve steps forward, detours, steps backward, rethinking and incorporating new ideas and behaviors and beginning again. The changes will be messy and require commitments to the ongoing process as we create and galvanize what is needed for sustainable peace.

The untried, unfamiliar ways must be explored and included.

What if we used artificial intelligence widely and systematically? Could we achieve lasting peace by incorporating the best features of AI? What is available? What has been tried? What needs to be added?

Imagine applying this experience from a recent article by Josh Bersin: *AI Unlocks New Power for Employees: Are HR Leaders Ready?* [13] What if we used the quadrants model which he proposes?

The first two explanatory quadrants are beneficial when the user needs the flexibility to ask questions to explore patterns dynamically or when the user is helped to absorb and define actions by discussing insights from data conversationally via interactive chat.

---

[13] https://sloanreview.mit.edu/article/ai-unlocks-new-power-for-employees-are-hr-leaders-ready/

The sophisticated quadrants are valuable when users need to explore insights dynamically and to compare notes across multiple influencing factors as well as to inform, influence with evidence, and inspire action.

Flexibility, insights, interaction, missing pieces, influencing factors – combine the best of human practices with AI?

Ready to try?

Lauryn Oates - Canada

Lauryn Oates advocates for equitable access to quality education in conflict zones and works to realize the transformative power of educated women and girls. She is Executive Director of Right to Learn Afghanistan, a charity that has helped make the human right to education real for Afghan women and girls through DD Academi, a virtual school, and other education programs that have ensured access to learning for thousands of Afghan girls and women.
www.righttolearn.ca

Education Builds Humanity

Nearly a century ago, Jean Piaget said "Only education is capable of saving our societies from possible collapse, whether violent or gradual." This statement is as true today as it was then. Education is the primary means by which global peace can be achieved. But not just any education.

It's critical that progress be made on the still dramatically high number of children and youth who are out of school: some 250 million. But access itself is not enough. What is most promising for peace is the potential for schooling to nurture agency and free thinking. When this happens on a mass scale, schools produce problem solvers and peacemakers, who collectively, can transform their societies. Yet, in much of the world, we have not yet realized approaches to education capable of achieving this.

While there's much discussion of the need for peace education, this is often approached as something that can simply be added to existing curricula. I'm calling for something far more transformative -- even disruptive – that requires a completely different way of thinking about the purpose and potential of education.

The world needs education systems that foster critical thinking, at every level of education, and in teacher education. We need schools where children learn to ask questions, more than memorize content. Where they can freely express themselves, more than stick to safe scripts. Where they can imagine, invent, and innovate, more than replicate existing systems. We need education that emboldens dissenters, celebrates heterodoxy, promotes intellectual diversity and divergence, and rewards moral courage and risk-taking and rigorous thinking – rather than just rigorous study.

The world's need for critical thinking is demonstrated by the role that dogma, extremism and indoctrination play in fuelling violence, and consequently, war. The dream of peace is inseparable from the dream of pluralism, of tolerance and of societies where people from every walk of life can think and act freely, without fear. In too many parts of the world, this is not the case. And it happens that those same places are often where violent conflict seems endemic. They also happen to be the same places where the status of women is poor, with all the tragic outcomes of this: higher infant and child mortality, higher maternal mortality, poorer health indicators, poverty, lower educational attainment rates, high corruption and weak governance. There is overwhelming evidence that the status of women has an indisputable causal relationship with all of these socioeconomic scourges and more.

Ensuring access to education for women and girls is one place to start. But on its own, it's not enough. What really matters is what people are learning, and consequently, what they can do as a result of their education. Can they challenge the status quo? Can they reshape social norms that are limiting or harmful? Can they promote peaceful futures?

Ultimately, everyone – girls and boys, men and women – need access to the kind of education that builds humanity, rather than breaks and divides it, that opens and transforms minds, inoculates individuals from bad information and bad ideas, and nurtures questioners, innovators and free thinkers. These are the people who will conceive and carry out solutions for peace, and the world urgently awaits them.

Michael Chew - Australia

Michael Chew is an environmentalist, action-researcher, and photographer/designer with degrees in participatory design, social ecology, art photography, critical theory and mathematical physics. He is a Rotary Peace Fellow and passionate about the intersections between peace and the environment. His international perspectives come from involvement in a range of grassroots global solidarity initiatives: co-founding the NGO Friends of Kolkata to coordinate international volunteer programmes and teach participatory photography; working in Bangladesh on community-based climate adaptation; co-founding the Friends of Bangladesh climate justice solidarity group. He recently completed an action-research PhD exploring how participatory photography can inspire environmental behaviour change across Bangladesh, China and Australia. He runs the small consultancy Ecoimagine specializing in community-based research, creative participation, facilitation and program design.

www.ecoimagine.org

Peace Ecology

We currently stand at a critical juncture in humanity's evolutionary journey where peace and environmental harmony can show a pathway beyond our entrenched conflicts. The concept of Peace Ecology emerges as a hopeful beacon, illuminating our environment's capacity to inform and sustain peace. This paradigm shift urges us to embrace an ecocentric perspective, acknowledging and acting from our deep interconnectedness with nature.

To nurture peace ecology, we must address the spiritual crisis at the heart of our environmental challenges. Our current paradigm, rooted in egocentric leadership and a dualistic worldview, has blinded us to our deep interdependence with nature. We have commodified life itself, viewing the natural world as a mere resource, rather than our living home that deserves reverence.

The path forward demands a profound shift in consciousness. We must cultivate an ecocentric mindset that sees nature as an integral part of our being, and vice versa. This perspective echoes indigenous wisdom around the world, reminding us that true prosperity and peace flourish when we honour our responsibilities to the natural world.

Environmental peacebuilding initiatives demonstrate the power of ecological cooperation to bridge divides. From shared water stewardship to transboundary conservation areas, these efforts show that caring for our common home catalyses lasting peace.

The journey towards environmental peace begins within each of us. We are called to rebuild our personal relationship with nature, cultivating gratitude for its gifts. This intimate connection transforms our perspective, helping us see the world as an interconnected living organism.

For the younger generation, this shift is crucial. Children, with their innate wonder and connection to nature, can be powerful agents of change. By nurturing their bond with nature and fostering eco-psychological awareness, we can cultivate ecocentric leaders for a harmonious future.

Our actions now will shape the world our descendants inherit. Every choice we make is an opportunity to align with nature's rhythms and contribute to a more peaceful world.

We stand on the shoulders of visionaries like Wangari Maathai, whose Green Belt Movement linked environmental conservation and peace. Initiatives like EcoPeace Middle East inspire us, bringing diverse communities together to protect shared environmental heritage.

The path to peace is inseparable from our journey towards environmental harmony. As we cultivate an ecocentric mindset, embrace indigenous wisdom, and step into a deeper connection with nature, we lay the foundation for a truly sustainable peace.

In Thomas Berry's words, when we achieve "the proper relation" between "the curvature of the universe, the curvature of the Earth, and the curvature of the human," we'll reach "the celebratory experience that is the fulfillment of earthly existence." [14] This is the promise of ecocentric peace - a world where humanity lives in balance with nature, conflicts transform through shared stewardship, and every action nurtures the web of life connecting us all.

The journey begins with each of us, as we choose to see ourselves as integral parts of Earth's magnificent tapestry. In this recognition lies the seed of lasting peace - for our communities, our world, and future generations.

---

[14] From Brian Swimme and Thomas Berry, "*The Universe Story: From Primordial Flaring Forth to the Ecozoic Era – A* *Celebration of the Unfolding of the Cosmos* (pp 261), Harper, San Francisco, 1992.

Todd MacLean - Canada

Todd MacLean is a writer, journalist and musician based in Prince Edward Island, Canada. He is the creator/editor of Global Chorus: 365 Voices on the Future of the Planet, an anthology of responses from leading global thinkers on our environmental future on Earth, and he is currently at work on his next project. As a busy award-winning musician as well, Todd is a multi-instrumentalist who performs frequently on the vibrant Atlantic Canadian music scene.

www.toddmaclean.com

Within Love Lies Our Hope

For tens of thousands of years on this Earth, humanity has been winning the game of survival of the fittest; but if we are to continue to survive on this planet, the name of humanity's new game needs to be "Survival of the Fairest."

Here are the truths that shape this game:

- As an individual, if I know that you are suffering, my peace is diminished, and therefore I must do what I can to help alleviate your suffering to help restore peace for you, peace for me, and peace for all.

- As a community, if we know that another community is suffering, our peace is diminished, and we therefore must do what we can to help alleviate their suffering to help restore peace for them, peace for us, and peace for all.

- As a human species, if we know that another species is suffering because of our own human actions, our peace is diminished, and we, therefore, must do what we can to help alleviate that species' suffering to help restore peace for them, peace for us, and peace for all.

If humanity as a global community can learn to guide the social evolution of our species toward adopting the framework of this new game of life as described, then we have the hope of living sustainably and peacefully on Earth for as long as this planet will provide the conditions for life as we need it.

Survival of the fittest – fighting hard for our way to the top – brought us to where we are: at the summit of the food chain, and dominating, but now, unfortunately resulting in our own degradation and hardship. So, we need to learn that we don't need to fight anymore.

Survival of the fairest means that if we truly learn to embody the all-important spirit of compassion and live our lives in uncompromising fairness toward others – whether these others are other individuals, communities, races, religions, countries, or species – then we will succeed in being everything we could ever dream of becoming as the beautiful human species that we are.

We'll never find the peace and sustainability that we seek as humanity if Love does not lead the way:

Within Love resides our hope. And if every generation tries to Love this Earth, and one another, a little more than the last, one of these generations we're going to get it right.

Chapter Seven: Global Considerations

If we are serious about peace, then we must work for it as ardently, seriously, continuously, carefully, and bravely as we have ever prepared for war.
– Wendell Berry (Writer, poet, activist, 1934 – present, USA)

When, in 2016, I co-organized the global initiative Women's Peace Tables Worldwide, women in more than 120 settings around the world stepped up to organize a peace table event. These events ranged from small groups around a table in an office lunchroom to hundreds of people in an auditorium, with the tables providing a space in which a community could speak to the challenges to peace they were facing.

Each table produced a report outlining what they addressed and the decisions that needed to be made. Most of the identified threats to peace, causes of conflict, and possible solutions were universal or had implications on a global level.

Although the potential for conflict and crises exists and is realized in discreet regions of the world, the causes, consequences, and responses to conflict are global and, understanding them requires us to think beyond peacebuilding projects to the interaction between issues and circumstances such as development, climate change, militarization, food insecurity, and systemic and cultural discriminatory practices and policies. When considering how to create a world in which peace is possible and where the potential for conflict is reduced, the peacebuilding lens must be broad and inclusive.

This chapter presents varying perspectives on issues that affect the globe as well as steps that could be taken to lead the world, as a whole, to a more peaceful state. The peacebuilders contributing here tackle militarization/demilitarization, the weapons industry, weapons control and disarmament, the role of the United Nations, and the intersection between peace and conflict and climate change, food insecurity, poverty, and health.

> *In a world in which all problems are global, there is no way countries*
> *can handle issues by themselves; we need global responses.*
> – António Guterres, UN Secretary-General

Irene Santiago - Philippines

Irene Santiago is a woman of many parts: groundbreaker, peacemaker, a warrior for women's equality in Asia and the Pacific. A native of the Philippines, she was instrumental in the implementation of a peace agreement that ended a 50-year conflict in her native Philippines. In 1995, she led the NGO Forum on Women as part of the UN World Conference on Women in Beijing—the largest and most important global gathering for women's empowerment to date. In 2005, she was one of 1000 women who were nominated for the Nobel Peace Prize.

The Awesome 'AND'

To me, peacebuilders should carry clear, simple and actionable concepts in their bag every day. With all the crises of gargantuan proportions we are experiencing, I would like to suggest a clear, simple concept.

I begin with a question. What is the most devastating word in the English language? It is a two-letter word. That's all. But because of that two-letter word, the world has experienced horrific cases of genocide, war, the most brutal atrocities, and never-ending violence.

That two-letter word is 'OR'. Me or you. Us or them. My country or your country. My religion or your religion. My truth or your truth. For some reason we are wired to think that someone or some people have to be superior, others inferior; some strong, others weak; some smart, others stupid; some winners, others losers; some saved, others damned to eternal fire.

So, what is the antidote to the Devastating 'OR'?

It's a three-letter word. I call it the Awesome 'AND'. Me and you. Us and them. My country and your country. My religion and your religion. My truth and your truth. We are ALL superior, strong, smart, winners, saved.

Yes, the power of our connectors. The idea that nobody and nothing stands alone, and we can all live in peace with each other and with nature. As women, we have tremendous capacities to connect. We therefore have our work cut out for us, and for men too.

As I see the various crises play out in the world today upending many lives and futures – the climate crisis, the health crisis, the economic crisis – it is easy to be overwhelmed and to retreat to our little corner of the world where life is more manageable and under our control. It is as though the smaller our world is, the safer we seem to feel from the ravages of global destruction.

However, in critical times, peacebuilders know that there are two things needed to keep people living and thriving. We know this because in times of peace, there are two things in abundance: hope and trust.

With hope we can dream, we can act. With trust, we can dream together, we can act together. In a world faced with crises on many fronts, we have to hold on to hope. But we have to build the 'AND' together, to trust one another in a never-ending circle of connections until we build the Beloved Community that Dr. Martin Luther King, Jr. envisioned for humanity.

Maiden Manzanal-Frank - Canada

Maiden Manzanal-Frank is a global impact adviser who works with governments, nonprofits, businesses and international organizations to achieve their impact locally and internationally. She aligns leaders and executives of on-purpose organizations to their singular objective so that they can do more good in the world. She is the founder and CEO of GlobalStakes Consulting, a Rotary Peace Fellow, writer, instructor, and mentor to aspiring start-ups and social innovators.

Bringing People Together for Peace

When good people stand up and own the problems of disintegration, polarization, and conflicts in their communities, then finding a way to peace is possible.

There are many people who ignore the early warning signs of social disintegration because they believe that it will just go away. History is replete with cases where it was too late for authorities and social advocates to stop the advances of radicalism or conflict because these issues grew incrementally. "We didn't know that it would happen this way," is what we hear all the time.

The more people are aware that they can take action to prevent these conflagrations, the better for long-term management of these issues. Tackling these at a smaller level will create positive ripple effects for mediation and restoring confidence measures.

At the societal level, there is a need to go beyond the victim-victimizer/oppressor-oppressed paradigm to see both conflicting parties as humans and not demonize one another for the sake of downplaying their humanity and justifying violence as a way to deal with differences.

When people become enlightened about the real issues without the propaganda, misinformation, and biased perspective, then they can make intelligent decisions operating on common ground and not a zero-sum worldview of economies and politics.

There is no peace without justice.

You can create lasting peace in communities when the issues that drive people apart begin to close as a result of dialogue, working together, and commitment despite decades-long antagonism and differences.

There must be a moral clarity on what is acceptable and not acceptable in our modern civilization. If we allow lawlessness, violence, and bigotry to rule our institutions and dominate our social consciousness, then this will open the floodgates of more violence and less peace.

We can put civility back in our social conversations about the many issues that beset our societies. Sad to say, we're not listening anymore to each other but out-talking one another through social media and that doesn't help.

We can arrange debates and propositions of new ideas that put the role of ethics, morality, and spirituality back on the table in our workplaces, schools, organizations, and networks.

This is possible if we're not afraid to hold these spaces and become facilitators for communicating change.

Keya Nicholas - Uganda

Keya (Nemesis) Nicholas is a musician, entrepreneur in the music and technology sector, and co-founder of EnterAfrica, a creative trans-African organization with the goal of enhancing living conditions through art and technology. He also works as a social activist with Viva con Agua to provide access to clean drinking water and basic sanitation for all worldwide.

Acting with Intention

The creation of systems, attitudes, and environments that foster equity, justice, empathy, and cooperation on every level, especially the individual and family levels, is a sustainable path to global peace.

Individuals in every state must understand:

Who said the wicked must pay?

Who said benevolence pays?

Every individual vote and economic transaction give power and voice to either benevolent or wicked practices and individuals. We are all response able but are mostly reactive.

All instruments of physical violence - weapons and troops - must be controlled and awarded on moral merit by an international body because social tensions lead again and again to warlike actions derailing the cultivation of global cooperation.

We live ever increasingly in a world affected by the forces of globalization indicating

that socially at least, coexistence of diverse societies is possible.

Hence, units of power within states must always be ready to settle differences of interest without force of arms - and the same is true of interstate relations - by leveraging global economic policies and actions aimed at tackling poverty, improving access to education, and addressing the systemic inequalities in wealth distribution.

Globally supervised state progressive taxation, support for local economies, sustainable business practices, and greater investments in healthcare and education will incentivise national policy changes and support fair trade practices internationally.

The fears aroused by social tensions threatening violence can often be discharged by an international body wielding the monopoly of military action and direct physical force and assuming the role of supreme regulator for larger units of inner and interstate dependencies.

States adhering to international laws and bodies of governance must consolidate this power by growing functional interdependencies amongst themselves, overseen by the overarching international body. In this way, diplomacy, multilateral cooperation, committed global solution efforts towards climate change, resource depletion, and nuclear disarmament are enforced.

The long-term well-being of humanity must be the core goal.

This dynamic can transform interstate social relationships and social fears slowly cease to become trumpets of warring factions.

This point of view illuminates the current ambivalent process that increases the privileges of member states and suggests that by stabilizing trade, security, and sovereignty relations, it offers a way to bring an end to the warrior societies and their remote pressures which cascade into global conflicts of conquest.

In the wake of this pacification, inner fears of one sector grow in proportion to the decrease of outer fears and states start to experience each other in a more differentiated way as the constraint of state self-control increases.

Rogue warring states must be globally defeated collectively, and the shock of defeat and loss suffered will pacify the entire international structure with long-lasting effects.

The international body's member states must contain within themselves the agitation aroused by the constant tug of war resulting from interstate relations.

"To draw a fate, reason needn't a trace" - Keya Nicholas

Human societies must be intentional about the structure of justice, cross-cultural dialogues, challenges to discriminatory practices, and support of policies that prioritize equality and inclusion.

Jane Murutu - Kenya

Jane Murutu is a Rotary Peace Fellow living and working in Kenya. Jane is an accomplished Project Manager. She has worked for Konrad Adenauer Stiftung- Kenya for 9 years. Her specialty is in Governance, Policy and Conflict Resolution. She holds a BA from Moi University and an MA from Kampala International University.

Peace is in Our Hands

Achieving global peace requires a multifaceted approach addressing societal, political, economic, and cultural factors. At the core lies fostering empathy, understanding, patience, and cooperation among individuals and nations.

Learning to truly listen, understand, and re-frame differences and concerns are vital skills for peacebuilding. The art of reframing helps conflicting parties to look at, and understand, conflict in a more open-minded and hopeful way.

These skills open the door for non-violent responses. This means actively responding to situations with patience and understanding, rather than aggression or anger. By embodying nonviolence, we contribute to a culture of peace, setting an example for others to follow in our societies.

If we are to build peace at the global level a culture of peace and promoting diplomacy and international cooperation is imperative. Building strong partnerships, resolving disputes peacefully, and adhering to international law can prevent conflicts from escalating and promote peaceful resolutions.

This includes respecting each nation's sovereignty. The so-called "superpowers" should not engage in careless selling of arms, or forge war allies but instead be purveyors of peace and strictly adhere to international laws.

To effectively prevent wars and promote global peace, the African Union (AU) and other United Nations (UN) bodies should adopt a comprehensive, proactive, and cooperative approach that addresses the root causes of conflict, strengthens institutions, and fosters collaboration.

At the local level, we can champion peace in schools, embedding peace subjects in the curriculum, training more mediators at each strata of society, and investing more resources in conflict resolution and peacebuilding.

Ultimately, "It may seem sometimes as if a culture of peace does not stand a chance against the culture of war, the culture of violence and the cultures of impunity and intolerance. Peace may indeed be a complex challenge, dependent on action in many fields and even a bit of luck from time to time. It may be a painfully slow process, and fragile and imperfect when it is achieved. But peace is in our hands. We can do it." - Kofi Annan

---

Tireless supporters have tried to make a difference one act of kindness, one act of solidarity, one act of charity at a time. They did so because they believe all humans are born free and equal in dignity and rights. They believe in acting toward one another in a spirit of humanity because human rights are universal, and justice and peace are human rights.
- Widad Akreyi from her acceptance speech, Pacem in Terris Peace and Freedom Award (2017)

Elaine Pratley - Australia

When **Elaine Pratley** first moved from her native Malaysia to Switzerland, she was taken aback by how hard it was to make friends. She was an awkward 13-year-old and unable to speak the local language. One winter day, a boy approached her with a sandwich and invited her to share his meal. That act of compassion began Elaine's lifelong journey of using food to promote peace between people of different ages, cultures, and beliefs in the various countries she has called home, whether Malaysia, New Zealand, China, Thailand, or Australia. Elaine is a lawyer, social entrepreneur, and peace advocate living and working in Melbourne, Australia. She is associated with the Monash Global Peace and Security (GPS) Centre and the Founder of Peace Inc. and Peace Kitchen.

www.peaceinc.com.au   www.peacekitchen.com.au

Food and Peace: The Need for a Global Food Peace Agenda

The world is facing a global hunger crisis. Ironically, we have the resources to feed everyone. To fix our broken food system, we need a global food peace agenda that mobilizes people across borders.

When considering the relationship between food and conflict, it is evident that widespread hunger exacerbates violent conflict. However, it may surprise many to learn how easily human-induced conflict can trigger food insecurity, even in regions with abundant food resources.

For instance, armed forces often manipulate food insecurity for strategic gain by blocking food aid or destroying food stocks, farmlands, and machinery, creating food shortages in opposition-controlled areas. Unfortunately, weaponizing starvation and depriving the hungry is one of the oldest tactics of warfare.

An effective food peace agenda must address such human-induced food insecurity and also respond to existential threats posed by weather and climate extremes—like flooding, bushfires, and rising sea levels.

These events put global food systems at significant risk. Beyond food insecurity, a food peace agenda must consider food's social relations: just as the absence of food can cause social divisions, its presence can create bonds. Who gets to eat and who does the cooking have long been the focus of feminist research. Sociologists have also explored how food encounters and 'smelly food' can give rise to racism and prejudice.

Encouragingly, eating together has the potential to foster social bonds, sometimes even with adversaries.

A global food peace agenda must push the boundaries of how we commonly understand 'conflict'. Our relationship with food is not just a social matter but intertwined with issues like environmental conflict, sustainability, and food waste. For many, our meat consumption is a moral and religious concern given how it entails animal violence. Studying food prompts us to think about peace and conflict expansively.

Food's many entanglements highlight the need for a global food peace agenda. Conflicts in regions like Gaza and Ukraine show how easily armed violence can disrupt global food chains. Including other forms of food conflict—whether social, existential, environmental, or moral—makes it clear that global peace requires collective effort.

What and how we eat offers much food for thought on how to promote peace in our interconnected world.

Global Partners in Peace Rotary Club - Worldwide

The **Global Partners in Peace Rotary Club** consists of Peace Fellow alumni, former Rotary youth exchange students and youth leaders, former Interact and Rotaract members, and partners in peace, including individuals who belong to other organizations and contribute to peacebuilding.

Providing Space for a Global Dialogue

In order to approach our understanding of the collective action toward peace, we invite you to consider three key points with which we have built roads, bridges and global dialogues.

As the first point of action, when speaking about humanity, as a collective movement, we understand that the concept of peace goes beyond our own understanding of the deep relationships that have historically been established with beings beyond the human and includes nature as a living territory.

Our club has broken away from the constraints of geography and we find ourselves building paths to peace from different countries and continents. Thanks to the plurality of understandings about what peace and community mean, we have asked ourselves what are the visions that we share and what differentiates us about this vision.

We have reached a consensus on the importance of reestablishing the relationships that we have between land, nature, societies and cultures. We recognize that when speaking about the contextualization of peace it also makes sense to talk about structural violence such as racism, colonialism, patriarchy and the conflict between human beings and nature.

Secondly, we have asked ourselves a question related to our individual and collective thinking: how can we weave community into our perspective when we name ourselves as global partners for peace?

We are faced with a growing debate in peacebuilding related to the need for places of care in which there can be careful communication and collective action through building consensus and considering the importance of affections and emotions in the work we do - from day-to-day conversations to the implementation of projects.

The two previous action points constitute part of the definition of our "partners" concept. To complement the learning circle of our work, we need a way of reconstructing paths: valuing dialogue as a form of action that transcends the dynamics of human and natural relationships.

As a collective, we are deepening our ability to facilitate dialogues that mobilize diverse participants towards personal and collective transformation. These dialogues provide an opportunity for learning and being open to the ethical-political debate between those that participate in each action.

We hope that sharing what we do, and who we are as a collective, provides an example of an important political act in peacebuilding. We consider that access to information, its flow and the sense it has for a world with constant questions is vital to continuing to weave the paths towards the diverse and different ways of making peace.

Marianne Hanson - Australia

Marianne Hanson is an Associate Professor of International Relations. She gained her master's and doctoral degrees at Oxford University and has taught in the fields of international security, human rights, and international law for three decades. She is currently Co-Chair of ICAN Australia (International Campaign to Abolish Nuclear Weapons), which was awarded the Nobel Peace Prize in 2017 for its efforts to raise awareness of nuclear dangers and its role in persuading states to adopt the UN Treaty on the Prohibition of Nuclear Weapons.

Collective Action in Peace

My 30 years of experience as an academic specialising in global peace and security, including as Foundation Director of the University of Queensland's Rotary Peace Centre in Brisbane, Australia, has led me to the following conclusions: first, there are endless numbers of wonderful individuals who are dedicated to peace and conflict resolution. I have had the pleasure of meeting several of these people through the Rotary Peace Fellowship program.

Second, while I applaud their work and the commitment of Rotary, I think we need to look at some of the long-standing obstacles that are making peace very difficult to achieve at the moment.

I am thinking here of the vested interests that are having a growing impact on policymaking; this is leading to government decisions which create more violence and inequality.

Unless we address the very serious problem of how weapons manufacturers strive to keep wars going, how the fossil fuel industry jeopardises our chances of addressing climate change successfully, how the 'revolving-door' practice influences politics (whereby many of our politicians routinely sit on the Boards of weapons corporations, or profit from donations by fossil fuel companies), and how the domination of mainstream media often brings us only a limited or one-sided picture of conflicts, it is hard to move towards peace.

I see a worrying deterioration of democracy. Even in the so-called advanced democracies of Australia, Europe, the United States, etc., it is getting harder to move beyond these vested interests, and the wishes of the people are increasingly ignored in favour of short-term political goals and economic enrichment for the few.

Most people want peace. But for me, the massive growth of the military-industrial-political complex is the biggest challenge we face today.

Yet at times like these, it is important to remember that people can change the world.

Without the mass actions of people who have spoken up against slavery, inequality, militarism and racism, etc., change would not have come about as it has.

My most pressing concern is the growing risk of nuclear warfare: we must take every step we can to abolish these weapons of mass destruction. We've outlawed chemical and biological weapons as abhorrent and inhumane; it is now time to eliminate nuclear weapons.

People have the agency to demand this of their governments. Nuclear weapons could wipe us all out; that is why even so-called 'conservative' leaders like Ronald Reagan and William Perry have called for the elimination of all nuclear weapons.

Rallying against the weapons manufacturers is vital for this cause and as people committed to peace, we must rise to this challenge.

We must never give up hope that change is possible and that we all have the agency to make that change happen, even if there are impediments that stand in our way.

Murwarid Ziayee - Canada/Afghanistan

Murwarid Ziayee is a dedicated advocate for women's rights and social justice in Afghanistan, with over two decades of experience working for gender equity, human rights, and women's empowerment. Her extensive work in conflict environments has equipped her with unique insights and resilience, which she channels into her advocacy efforts. Through her writing, Murwarid aims to inspire others to contribute to global peace.

Sowing the Seeds of Peace

For humanity to achieve peace on a global scale, several crucial factors must align. Understanding and addressing root causes of conflict such as inequality, injustice, and resource scarcity, often rooted in supremacy, is essential.

History serves as a valuable guide, showing how notions of supremacy fueled many wars and conflicts, be it in religious, ideological, or racial contexts.

To tackle supremacy, fundamental reforms within global education systems are necessary. Education must foster empathy and understanding among individuals, communities, and nations through dialogue, cultural exchange, and education emphasizing common humanity over divisions.

Educating future generations to honor and appreciate the beliefs, values, and cultures of other nations is imperative to cultivate mutual respect and understanding, laying the groundwork for a more harmonious world.

In the pursuit of global peace through political avenues, we must redefine the notion of "justice" on a global scale. Justice must transcend subjective or relative values, embodying an absolute value that requires courage to uphold, even at the cost of personal interests.

By prioritizing fairness and equity globally, we can foster an environment where mutual respect and cooperation flourish, contributing to lasting peace.

Effective governance structures prioritizing diplomacy, cooperation, and conflict resolution are key, as well as strengthening international institutions like the United Nations and freeing them from superpower influence.

Once liberated and acting as an independent body, the UN can assume a significant role in resolving conflicts worldwide, being regarded with the seriousness it deserves.

While these reforms are essential steps toward creating peace, the most crucial reforms stem from within us, from our hearts.

If every individual on this planet could internalize the wisdom of Rumi's words when he says "In this earth, in this earth, in this pure farm, let's sow nothing, but the seeds of love and kindness" then our world would be free from conflicts and wars.

Peace may be hard to achieve but is possible with small yet essential steps that are guided by courage and sufficient commitment.
- Widad Akreyi

Voice of Women for Peace – Canada

Voice of Women for Peace (VOW) advocates for a holistic approach to global peace, emphasizing the interconnectedness of social justice, environmental sustainability, disarmament, and active non-violence. We believe in the critical importance of amplifying the voices of marginalized communities, particularly women, Indigenous peoples, and other historically oppressed groups, as indispensable contributors to authentic peacebuilding. These perspectives hold the key to creating sustainable and lasting peace.

www.vowpeace.org

A Holistic Approach to Global Peace

There is an urgent need for disarmament, beginning with the abolition of nuclear weapons: weapons that pose an existential threat to humanity and the planet. The Treaty on the Prohibition of Nuclear Weapons is highlighted as a crucial step toward this goal. The treaty's success depends on grassroots movements that pressure governments to sign and rigorously implement it. Community engagement in peace education, which highlights the catastrophic consequences of nuclear warfare and promotes non-violence, is essential in maintaining peaceful relations and holding governments accountable for their commitments to peace.

Disarmament is not just about reducing the threat of nuclear conflict; it also has profound environmental implications. Military activities are significant contributors to environmental degradation, causing pollution, habitat destruction, and resource depletion. By redirecting military expenditures toward sustainable development and climate change mitigation, we can address these issues at their core. Prioritizing disarmament can reduce the ecological footprint of military operations and reallocate resources to renewable energy, conservation projects, and green technologies. Environmental education and community-led conservation efforts are crucial in empowering local populations, fostering a culture of peace, and promoting environmental stewardship.

The interconnectedness of disarmament and environmental sustainability is evident; progress in one area reinforces the other, creating a positive feedback loop that benefits both the planet and its inhabitants.

Peace cannot exist without addressing systemic inequalities and injustices. Advocacy for the rights of marginalized communities, ensuring equal access to resources, and dismantling oppressive structures are all critical components of this effort. VOW's involvement in the international lobby for Security Council Resolution 1325 on Women, Peace, and Security is a testament to the importance of inclusive peace processes. Governments must take concrete action to implement such resolutions, ensuring that women and marginalized groups play central roles in conflict prevention and resolution.

Building a culture of peace requires nurturing relationships based on empathy, respect, collaboration, and cooperation, beginning at the community level. Local initiatives can create spaces for dialogue and understanding, fostering a deeper sense of connection and shared purpose. Peace education programs that teach conflict resolution, promote intercultural understanding, and emphasize non-violent communication are vital in instilling these values in daily life. By fostering these principles, we lay the groundwork for a more peaceful, just, and sustainable world.

We need to build a multifaceted strategy that integrates disarmament, social justice, and environmental sustainability if we are to build a peaceful, just, and sustainable world. Organizations like VOW exemplify how advocacy and community engagement can drive meaningful change. Through collective action and holistic peacebuilding, humanity can create a world where peace, justice, and environmental stewardship coexist harmoniously.

Rebwar Mohamed Salih currently lives in the Sulaymaniyah, Kurdistan region of Iraq where he grew up witnessing many wars, including the eight years of the Iraq/Iran war, the first and second Gulf Wars, and numerous civil wars before and after the US invasion of 2003. Rebwar studied teaching in Sulaymaniyah and International Relations in London, England. Then, following the mass influx of Syrian refugees to the Kurdistan region of Iraq following the Arab Spring uprising, began working with refugees for INGOs and UNHC. He is a Rotary Peace Fellow and achieved his master's degree in Peace and Conflict Studies at the University of Queensland in Australia in 2023.

Coming Together for a Common Goal

The concept of peace is very broad. It may have a different meaning for different people in different parts of the world.

When I think about peace, I wonder, "Whose peace?" and a question naturally comes to my mind: "is the meaning of peace the same for someone in a tiny island state in the Pacific, in central Asia, in a rural area in Latin America, a nomad in Mongolia, the Indigenous people in Canada, the USA and Australia, or women in Saudi Arabia or Iran? Are civilians trapped in bunkers for months in Ukraine and Palestinians under continuous shelling from air, sea and land in Gaza thinking about peace in the same way people think about it in the developed world?"

The answer is not simple. Young Palestinians have seen many wars in their lives, while people in the developed world are concerned with issues surrounding health insurance, or high tax rates, or 40-hour work weeks. Mongolian nomads consider finding good pastures for their livestock to be their main concern. Native people around the world wish for the settlers to acknowledge the pain and suffering that they inflicted on them.

We don't know what it is like to lose our home, and everything passed down through the generations until it happens to us. When ISIS invaded large swathes of land in Iraq and Syria in 2014 thousands of middle-class families lost everything overnight and found themselves in IDP camps waiting in long lines to receive a meal provided by humanitarian agencies.

It is not easy to accomplish peace because peacemakers cannot compete against mass media - affiliated with powerful actors - that is designed to deceive and mislead people about what is going on throughout the world. Politicians, including those in the western democracies, have been effective in their efforts to divide people on the basis of ideological and religious beliefs in order to dominate them and maintain power.

However, there is possibility in a shared aspiration of millions of people around the world that ties all our hopes for peace together. Ordinary citizens around the world endure more or less the same sort of suffering and subjugation and therefore, we have the common struggle and a common goal: to achieve peace. Peacemakers have a long and bumpy road to go that requires tolerance and patience until peace is achieved.

I assert that if the society in the western world, in general, and citizens of the permanent members states of the Security Council, in particular, "want peace at home" they bear a heightened obligation to actively pursue peace on an international scale by actively opposing their governments in two specific ways: demanding that there be no collaboration with regimes that mistreat their populace on grounds of race and religion, and demanding that they stop the supply of weapons that are used on a large scale to kill civilians.

Selvi Roy - Canada

Selvi Roy is the Special Projects Coordinator at Chalice, one of Canada's largest child sponsorship organizations working in 50 sites across 13 countries to support more than 50,000 individuals, families, and communities in their efforts to overcome the cycle of poverty. Her professional background is in Social Work and Education with experience spanning 27 years in international settings where she worked in the fields of primary health, education, sustainable livelihood, and peace promotion. She is the Maritime Canada liaison for the International Cities of Peace initiative, which is associated with the United Nations Economic and Social Council (UN ECOSOC) and 412 cities of peace worldwide.

Be the Change You Want to See

You only live once! Of the 8.1 billion people in the world today, there is only one you. And never ever will there be another. This thought is coupled mesmerizingly with the insight that this moment is fleeting.

The ongoing Russia-Ukraine war, Israeli-Palestinian conflict, Taliban's violently oppressive regime in Afghanistan, and ongoing conflicts in Sudan, the Central African Republic, and Haiti, besides nuclear threats from North Korea and sporadic spikes in regional and local conflicts around the world, have only served to accentuate the need for peace.

According to the United Nations, internationally, nearly 120 million people were displaced due to violence and conflicts in 2023. Across Canada, the 874 homicides and 129,876 victims of violence that were reported in 2022, apart from the 15,074 violent, mostly hate propaganda-related crimes recorded in Winnipeg and the recently noted 24 shooting deaths in Toronto in the first half of 2024, do not fade out the still shocking shooting rampage in Portapique, Nova Scotia that left 22 persons dead, in 2020.

Amid hate-filled violence and resultant loss and grief, my heart, like many others', cries out for peace.

Growing up in India, just a few blocks away from where Mahatma Gandhi was shot and killed and bearing witness to the violent Hindu-Sikh riot in my neighborhood in November 1984, the horrors of hate-induced actions stay etched in my mind.

Years later, I learned from Richard Cuadra, Attitudinal Healing Coach, that fear is the antonym of love, not hate, and that giving is the same as receiving. Though I was initially confused, I knew that if I could work with someone needing peace, I, too, would gain peace through the process.

Every time I need to make a decision, especially one that may impact many people, as recommended by Mahatma Gandhi, I try to picture in my mind the face of the poorest and weakest person I know and ask myself if the decision will impact this person positively. Through this contemplation, I get my answer.

Fred Arment, of International Cities of Peace, has said there are more than 8 billion ways to promote peace.

And so, with the unfailing support and efforts of hundreds of peace supporters, Charlottetown, Prince Edward Island, became a member of the International Cities of Peace to continue each one's desire for peace in our communities and around the world.

Being a member of the International Cities of Peace, I stay encouraged to continue promoting peace in my own way - by doing what I can, when, where, and however I can.

"Be the change you want to see," said Mahatma Gandhi.

Ayesha Khan - Gilgit Baltistan, Pakistan

Ayesha Khan is a humanitarian and Global Goodwill Ambassador. She has worked in the education and empowerment of girls and women as the Chairperson of her organization GDWO, established the first 'Girls school' in the volatile area of Diamer in the Gilgit Baltistan region of Pakistan in 2012 and created homeschooling for wider outreach. Miss Khan has written articles in National and International newspapers about regional political development, the environment, women's empowerment and the status of Gilgit Baltistan. She is the first Chairperson for APCEA, Pakistan's first women empowerment Committee and is an Ambassador for Gilgit Baltistan for the international humanitarian NGO Al Khidmat Foundation Pakistan.

We Need Peace Now!

We are living in the world of global uncertainty, chaos in many parts of the world, wars and unrest. There is no better time for us to unite as one to protect our future and our world and to vow to leave behind a better world for our children. In order to bring humanity together and ensure peace we must work together and build a peace-loving force to combat hatred, disillusion and division among people, societies and nations globally.

To reach to a common ground, we can:

1. Discourage and halt the weaponization of the world. It's time for the world to cut down on deadly weapons and halt the purchase and selling of deadly arms to other nations.

2. Build long-term peace plans for specific regions, especially volatile regions, and use pressure groups to disseminate that knowledge.

3. Hold regular sessions, peace meetings, rallies and social media awareness programs about all upcoming peace-related events, plans and courses of action.

4. Hold seminars and facilitate interactions regularly with different people, cultures, and faiths to learn from each other and find a common bond.

5. Raise awareness about significant conflicts around the world and support the victims of conflict, the suppressed and the marginalized.

6. We must educate people about saying NO to violence of all kinds.

7. Spread peace and peaceful ideas and means through collaboration with diverse

and like-minded organizations, institutions and individuals.

Let's reach out and let's act as a combined force to promote peace, and work towards peaceful resolutions for the volatile world. Peace doesn't only mean to fight against wars, it also means to work to end famine, hunger, disease, poverty and so much more.

Each step we take collectively can save a life and give hope to someone far away and each victory we achieve is a triumph for the world. We must find local partners globally to empower ourselves and help communities rebuild their lives. After all, we are all here to help each other and all people deserve a peaceful and rewarding life.

Melanie Tomsons – Canada

Melanie Tomsons is the Executive Director of Never Again International - Canada, a youth-based NGO that fosters leadership skills empowering children in conflict zones to speak out against crimes against humanity. The organization strives to make Never Again a reality by stopping atrocities of gender-based violence in fragile contexts and preventing genocide and the exploitation of child soldiers. Melanie founded the charity to amplify the voices of youth in conflict zones to advocate for the Sustainable Development Goals and become global citizens. Melanie also consults in the fields of peacebuilding and conflict resolution, child soldiers, war-affected children and human rights.
www.neveragaininternationalcanada.org

The Road To Peace

Humanity will begin to find peace when it undertakes a transformative mental shift in its ways of thinking about itself and its place in the world. By embracing the African philosophy of Ubuntu - "I am because we are" - we can forge a brighter future that underscores the importance of empathy and compassion and propounds the interconnectedness of all human beings. Humanity must come together in a spirit of hopeful altruism to right injustices and inequities for all people.

True and authentic peace can only be achieved when we extend our sphere of care to supporting the inherent rights and dignity of every individual. By becoming global citizens, we will create a new world order where we truly embrace principles of social justice and protect human rights.

Sustainable peace will be achievable when humanitarian law and global justice are respected, and adhering to principles of ethics becomes the norm rather than the exception. When this occurs, humanity will be able to effectively band together to combat existential threats, such as nuclear proliferation, climate change and emerging risks to global health.

Humankind must reject unjust systems and speak for our common future. We need to replace our limited understanding of justice with one that is connected to compassion, peace and the ethics of non-violence. For humanity to thrive and coexist, everyone needs to become agents of positive change in society – this role is not just for elite figureheads. *Everyone* must become humanitarian goodwill ambassadors.

Humankind will forge a clear path to peace when we realize that it is incumbent on each of us to exemplify and embody principles of compassion, kindness and mercy at the global level.

Collective action at the ground level is what will create a critical mass towards peace. NGOs must work hand-in-hand with communities and cease competing with each other to advance the common good.

Dr. Denis Mukwege, a Congolese gynecologist working with survivors of sexual violence said, "We all have the power to change the course of history when the beliefs we are fighting for are right." Indeed, we can unite to find a path towards peace by saying 'no' to apathy and indifference and committing ourselves to advancing the cause of humanity.

Barriers to education must be eliminated at a global level so that the hope and enthusiasm of children is nurtured, and principles of compassion, peace, and mercy are learned at an early age. In particular, systemic barriers girls face in attending school must be expunged; education protects children from being recruited as child soldiers or child brides.

By cultivating seeds of peace in youth, humanity can realize its true potential. Young people can be engaged in making a lasting difference to make the world a better place. Grassroots peacebuilding organizations, such as Never Again International – Canada, foster global citizens by engaging vulnerable youth in social justice initiatives. Young people are encouraged to take action and create a positive sustainable impact for future generations, advance peace through justice and promote gender equality worldwide. Never Again youth advocate for genocide prevention, stopping the exploitation of child soldiers and eradicating sexual gender-based violence as a weapon of war. They come to recognize that together we can create a more peaceful, equitable and sustainable world where we celebrate our common humanity.

For humanity to find a way to peace for the world as a whole, humankind must band together to care for creation and the most vulnerable, raise our voices to lift up the voiceless, and recognize that we belong to each other. Let us seize this moment to advance human rights and sustainable peace for all.

Di Bretherton - Australia

Di Bretherton is an Adjunct Research Professor at Batchelor Institute. She recently retired as Convenor of Psychologists for Peace, an Interest Group of the Australian Psychological Society. Books she has edited include *Methodologies in Peace Psychology: Peace Research by Peaceful Means,* with Siew Fang Law, and *Peace Psychology in Australia*, with Nikola Balvin. Both books are in the Peace Psychology Book Series edited by Daniel Christie.

Lessons from Peace Psychology

I began my peace journey as a small child. My Auntie Di, for whom I am named, was a college student at the time. When I was growing up, she kept her peace puppets in my grandmother's shed. The biggest treat for me was to be allowed to play with them. I still find in my work that role play, or with young children, puppets, provides a wonderful way of unpacking conflict and peace.

Role play allows us to illustrate and explore deep abstract ideas in a way which is light-hearted and funny. We can experiment with different strategies and consider how our own behaviour may affect outcomes. We can reverse roles and take different perspectives. We can stop partway through to call on the audience to come up with various endings and share experiences and ideas in an imaginative way.

When I studied psychology in university there were no courses in peace and conflict studies, or at least none that I knew of, and

no career guidance for girls. In the 1960s we were expected just to fill in the time at university until we got married.

Many readers will be familiar with the disappointment some young people feel when they enrol in psychology courses, hoping to better understand themselves and others, only to find they are confronted with the "rats and stats" variety of psychology.

Unlike the "rats and stats" variety, peace psychology is explicitly value-driven: our aim is to better understand ourselves so we can improve the way in which we relate to each other and create a better world for future generations.

This is not to say we reject statistics: they can be a powerful tool. Peace psychology does overlap with more established forms of psychology in studying topics such as stereotypes, prejudice and social identity but perhaps differs in its emphasis on

196

praxis: on taking psychological findings out of classrooms and psychology laboratories into social environments and learning from the experience of peace educators, leaders and activists.

Gradually I was able to bring my life as a peace activist into my work as a psychologist and in the 1980s peace psychology was formally established as a subdiscipline of psychology by the American Psychological Association.

Peace psychology aims to promote the management or, more ambitiously, the transformation of conflict, without using coercion, threat or violence. It also explores the building of social, economic and political structures that create environments in which people can live and flourish together.

Peace psychology began as a movement against war, investigating questions such as "How do we define violence?" and "What are the root causes of violence?" but has matured into giving equal emphasis to positive approaches to creating and maintaining peace, and to processes of collective social change. As peace psychologists, we keep in mind that while violence might stem from personal factors, such as an abusive childhood, sometimes the pathology is in the system, not the individual.

Peace psychology emphasizes creating the conditions that enable and sustain healthy relationships, not only between individuals but also within and between communities, nations and the natural world.

Eleanor Gordon - Australia

Eleanor Gordon is the Director of Monash Global Peace and Security Centre (Monash GPS), Australia. She is a practitioner and scholar with 25 years of experience addressing conflict-related security, justice and gender issues, including in management and advisory positions with the UN and other organisations in conflict-affected environments.

Complex, Interconnected Threats to Peace Demand an Inclusive and Integrative Approach

Threats to peace and security are increasingly complex and interconnected. The climate crisis and forced migration and conflict are deeply intertwined, with each impacting and being impacted by each other, and constituting one of the most pressing global challenges. The climate crisis forcibly displaces people, which, in turn, can trigger other sources of insecurity, from armed conflict to trafficking and modern slavery. Likewise, armed conflict can feed, and be fed by environmental degradation and resource scarcity, organised crime and corruption, depleted or fragile states and communities, human rights violations and grievances, inequalities and development challenges, as well as forced migration.

A vicious circle can ensue with each threat feeding each other, leading to globalised, multi-layered, seemingly intractable polycrises.

Addressing the complex, interconnected nature of threats to peace and security demands innovative and interconnected thinking by people working together across diverse industry sectors and academic disciplines.

Typically, however, the way the international system and academia are set up hinders this collaborative way of working.

Our work often requires us to distinguish ourselves into specific sectors or disciplines. We develop distinct languages and modus operandi and position ourselves against or in competition with others.

However, if we are to better understand and respond to such complex, interconnected threats, we must find a way to draw from the skills and knowledge of a diversity of scholars, policymakers and practitioners. Moreover, it is critical that the skills and knowledge of those most directly affected by conflict and insecurity are valued in collaborative approaches to building global peace and security.

The threats posed by complex interconnected crises demand an urgent shift in the way we understand, respond to and seek to prevent or mitigate them. It demands a genuinely inclusive, integrative, collaborative and creative approach, drawing from a diversity of knowledge and skills and responding to the needs of those who are most at risk.

———————————————

Although Peace can be negotiated by governments, it is ultimately the responsibility of the people themselves to make it last. All of us have a role to play to create a world in which peace can flourish.

- Widad Akreyi

Vitoon Viriyasakultorn - Thailand

Vitoon Viriyasakultorn worked as the Deputy Director of the Rotary Peace Center in Bangkok until 2023. Before this his work involved capacity building and training in natural resources and water conflict management nationally and internationally.

How and What We Learn is Crucial to Building Peace

We cannot engender peaceful communities and societies, if we fail at home.

Socialization within the family is crucial to building peaceful societies. Children learn from their families how to respect and deal with differences in opinions, culture, beliefs, ideologies, or religions. When traumatized or neglected by their families, youths are more likely to be involved in anti-social activities, violent cases, and killings.

How children are educated is also key to building peace. Here, in Thailand, some political parties have quietly intervened in school education through biased teachers to teach children fake news and biased political ideologies, resulting in social unrest. In short, we need to start at the most basic social institutions - families and schools - to bring peace to our communities and our societies.

At the global level, the possibility of peace is influenced by global politics and, of course, it links to national interests and benefits. In the world's histories until now,

we see that many armed conflicts, civil wars, genocides, world wars, etc., were often led by corrupt country leaders, in the name of their national interests and benefits, which may or may not be true.

Having worked internationally for about 20 years in the field of peacebuilding and conflict management, I have observed and learned from my course participants and peace fellows that many current national conflicts and civil wars are the result of colonization in their histories. Most countries in the world have been influenced by Western thinking and concepts - especially the political ideology of Western Democracy and human rights - without contextualizing those western concepts to their own situations and culture.

I think many current national and global conflicts are caused by the different understandings of what democracy really means. We can also see that democracies are dying in many historically democratic countries, especially in the US. I think it is time that each country should learn and understand its own history, culture, and context and build up their own national capacity, instead of relying on some powerful countries, which often bring the less powerful countries into wars with them.

In short, I would say "Democracy cannot be copied and pasted, it has to be contextualized." We must start with ourselves. We need to reorient our thinking and attitudes to accept new things and differences, at the same time also value local and national culture/histories, to build up social harmony. I believe if we have this in place at the community level it will contribute to global peace.

Habib Ahmad - Pakistan

Habib Ahmad has over 23 years of experience in humanitarian aid, development, and peace. Currently, he works as a Country Director at Human Relief Foundation UK and as Regional Coordinator – Asia & Pacific at Rotary Peace Fellow Alumni Association (RPFAA). He holds a master's degree in Sustainable Humanitarian Action- from UCAM, Spain, an MPhil in peace & Conflict Studies, an MA Social Work and a master's degree in public administration, with extensive practical experience with high-profile INGOs, and donor agencies in Pakistan, Afghanistan, the UK, and Thailand.

We must Raise our Voices

This is a critical time in human history. All humans belong to one man and one woman. Now there is greater diversity in this world as people live in one place and belong to different castes, colors, creeds, faiths, and nationalities.

All religions claim that they promote peace in society and the world, yet there is a threat to peace within every society. There is a great influence of culture on every religion to the point that no religion is free from the influence of their respective culture. Every religion claims to be pure, rooted in heaven and considers their religion as peaceful, and still, there is little peace in the world.

It is the responsibility of every human to work for a better society and humanity. It is our primary duty to stand against those actions which challenge the foundation of humanity and human existence. We must stand against biases and discrimination based on race or skin color, etc. We must raise our voices.

It is crucial for peacebuilders to raise their voices, and when doing so, it must be different from a layperson's approach. We must promote non-violent peace-building measures, dialogue and discussion among the people, groups, communities, and nations.

Our role must be proactive; we can promote peace education to develop a greater understanding of diversity in different spheres of life.

World peace depends on how the more powerful groups and people act toward and approach the less powerful. World peace is dependent on equitable distribution of resources and sustainable development of underprivileged communities across the globe. If people are going to bed hungry or have no shelter, there is a greater threat to peace and the door to violence and war opens.

Our role is to advocate for those who are suffering from crises and who are suppressed. Through peacebuilding, we must work toward an interactive network of peace and development. Peace without development is not sustainable. For the promotion of peace in society, we must work for a justice-based system which considers all peoples. In this way, we will ultimately contribute to a greater, more peaceful system.

Rana Dajani - Jordan

Rana Dajani is a Yidan Global Fellow at Harvard Graduate School of Education and a professor of molecular biology at the Hashemite University in Jordan. Her area of expertise is epigenetics and biomarkers of trauma among refugees. She is a tireless supporter of building indigenous research capabilities in the developing world and creating a mentoring program to support women scholars in STEM that was recognized by the National Academy of Sciences. She is the founder of We Love Reading, a grassroots initiative to create changemakers in underserved communities by fostering a lifelong love of reading. A recipient of the UNESCO International Literacy Prize, We Love Reading has established more than 8,000 locally run libraries in over 70 countries. She has also been recognized as a Fulbright, Eisenhower, Robert Bosch, Ashoka and Yale Morse Fellow, is on the list of the 100 most influential Arab Women and has received the Jacobs social entrepreneur award, the Nansen UNHCR refugee award, and the Schwab Social Entrepreneur Award.

Be the Butterfly of Social Justice

We need today, more than ever, a new world structure that is equitable and representative. The world is experiencing atrocities, wars, climate change and natural disasters everywhere; all of which can be traced to human action. The impact of imperialism and capitalism has escalated to an unprecedented degree. The rise of the far right and the extreme polarization that we are experiencing globally is clearly present in what is happening in Palestine. It has become a litmus test for the way the global community responds to humanitarian crises. Attempts to bring about peace have not succeeded because they have not addressed the root of the problem.

We see today, under the litmus test of Palestine, the UN system failing terribly with colonizer countries overruling colonized countries in voting against a ceasefire; demonstrating that the UN system does not reflect the reality of the world's moral decisions as it claims to do. It is like we are seeing in real-time an enactment of native Indigenous settler colonization, slavery, global south colonization, all happening in front of our eyes today in the 21st century.

History indeed is repeating itself and we are living it; even though the UN system was supposedly developed with the intention to protect against genocides from ever happening again.

It has been assumed that social innovation is the solution to the root causes of challenges in the world today but all the social innovation in the world would have not helped Gaza. It is the presence of structural barriers based on power and money, not values of morality and ethics, which underlie poverty, inequality, and violence. "You can't separate peace from freedom because no one can be at peace unless he has his freedom." (Malcolm X)

We need activism, not social innovation, to solve the world's problems. We need lawyers, activists and storytellers to shift the narrative and remind us of our collective humanity. Dehumanization is the driving force behind many of the atrocities being committed in the world today. "True peace is not merely the absence of tension; it is the presence of justice." (Martin Luther King Jr.)

The tangible spirit of our shared humanity prevailing across the globe as we rise up against injustice is a testimonial that our collective humanity is very much alive. I am full of optimism that a hopeful future is possible despite the detrimental times in which we live. The issue of Palestine, as Kavita Ramas put it, has awakened the "Ummah" amongst us and has brought humanity together for a common purpose. This feeling of "Ummah" brings us together to think creatively of how to be united despite barriers. We are at the brink of something big, we are living history, we are creating history, and we have the opportunity to create something better for future generations, together.

We must not underestimate the simple actions of each one of us. As the chaos theory states, when a butterfly flutters its wings in one part of the world, a hurricane is formed beyond time and space. What is that simple action that we can do? It can be words of truth in the huge silent void or actions as simple as boycotting.

As Einstein said: "the world will not be destroyed by those who do evil but by those who watch them without doing anything."

Jean-Paul Chami - Lebanon

Jean-Paul Chami is a Lebanese Peacebuilding Advisor specializing in the systemic analysis of protracted conflicts. He has more than 15 years of experience in designing and managing peacebuilding and conflict transformation programs and interventions, facilitating social and political dialogue, and analyzing conflict and peace. In 2011 he founded the Peace Labs NGO and directed its programs until 2023. Recently, he founded Catalyze, a company specializing in understanding and accompanying transitions and peaceful change at the institutional and societal levels. To date, he has led more than 200 training workshops, courses, and lectures in the Arab region such as Lebanon, Iraq, Yemen, Jordan, Libya and Morocco on topics, concepts and skills related to conflict and peace. He holds two master's degrees, one in Peace and Conflict Studies from the European Peace University in Austria (2007) and another in International Relations from the Lebanese American University (2004).

The Pursuit of Durable Peace

In striving for peace, we must acknowledge that any system, including our international one, will never be perfect. Yet, every system needs a way to signal when it reaches a breaking point—a safeguard for humanity. This "ouch! button" is more than an idea of mine; it's a call for mechanisms, institutions, and procedures, such as early warning and early response (EWER) systems, which can detect the rising heat of conflicts before they turn violent. These mechanisms would need to be accessible and actionable at all levels of society, giving communities a means to respond proactively to brewing tensions. Peace, after all, should not be an afterthought—it should be woven into the fabric of our global and local institutions.

As a collective, it's also time we shift our perspective from the absence of war to the pursuit of durable peace (quoting the late prof. Johan Galtung). This is not peace as a temporary solution; it's peace built on a foundation of equity and justice, a process that continues long after the signing of treaties. Durable peace supports conflicted societies not only to end violence but to develop the resilience and structures needed for long-term stability, even if that means committing to accompany them for decades (quoting John-Paul Lederach saying that it often takes as long to address a conflict as the time it took to get created, he also often says that the unit of time measurement in the peacebuilding realm is the decade, NOT the year). Only when peace is nurtured with such commitment can it withstand the test of time.

However, fostering peace requires us to engage actively—even during the "boring" times (times when there is no overt violence). Without the urgency of visible conflict, peace can start to feel like a topic of abstract ideals. This is where the media plays an essential role, connecting society to the values and realities of peace, reinforcing why it matters. Likewise, education systems need to promote conflict literacy, encourage systemic thinking and raise awareness about the intricate ties between conflict, peace, and the structures that support or undermine them. When society understands that peacebuilding is a complex, interconnected process, it can approach the task with patience (a VERY important missing ingredient) and purpose.

True peace demands that we choose leaders who embody the values of peacebuilding — those who reject war as an option, who champion demilitarization and denuclearization, and who advocate for WMD-free zones. Leaders must commit to the principle that supplying weapons to nations in conflict perpetuates suffering. Our collective voice, in turn, must demand leadership that prioritizes diplomacy, even better, a real collective problem-solving culture, over makeovers, politics and aggression, resilience over force, and dialogue over division.

To bring peace to our world, our communities, and our societies, we must cultivate a mindset where peace is the constant goal, not a crisis-driven endeavor.

Helen Bishop - Northern Territories, Australia

Helen Bishop is a Kungarakan woman of the Northern Territory, Australia. Her academic focus has been on her professional ambition to enlarge procedural fairness, dispute resolution, problem-solving and participatory agreement making, specifically to enhance First Nation Australians' access to such services. Helen champions dispute resolution as a means of closing the gap in service provision, as a constructive tool to enable greater access to restorative justice, effective governance and peacebuilding practices. Helen formalised her deep interests in social equity and peacebuilding by obtaining a MA in Conflict Resolution and a Professional Certificate in Indigenous Research and Leadership. Her aim is to support methods and practices with First Nation Australians in navigating conflict and process managing disputes that would otherwise continue to see them in regular contact with the criminal justice systems; the police, courts, custodial services, family and children's services, and other challenging or intrusive social deterrents and exchanges.

Earth Peace for Her Children – An Indigenous Point of View

As our Mother Earth tirelessly spins, offering all that we need, we, in our advanced state, continue to create destructive contrivances that serve no meaningful purpose and our bond with her weakens.

Despite her unwavering generosity, we are still plagued by greed, envy, ego, and the pursuit of power; these distort our thinking and lead us to inhumane and selfish actions. Our mother Earth, with her children, suffers the consequences of our destructive actions—for she is bombed, drilled, polluted, and scarred by the very beings she nurtures.

In the beginning, our Ancestors wove sacred laws that bound the First Nations peoples of Australia to each other and to the land herself. These ancient laws nurtured profound connections, intertwining their existence to the very essence of the land's agency, connecting we beings to her languages, to the flora and fauna of our territories. Through ceremonies, dance, song, and stories, we honoured our Ancestors and our mother Earth, acknowledging her as the eternal nurturer who provided water, food, and shelter—the very foundations of life. To this day, she remains a revered figure, embodying the roles of carer and provider, sustaining her children with the gifts upon which all life depends.

In this vast, arid land now known as Australia, the absence of animals or the technology to easily corral or contain creatures like kangaroos, emus, or echidnas demanded a profound collective effort for successful hunting and gathering. Survival in this harsh, unyielding landscape hinged on the unity and cooperation of entire land groups.

As conflicts inevitably arose, the Ancestors, with their deep wisdom, crafted intricate social arrangements to moderate discord. They devised systems that intricately intertwined flora, fauna, and people into a web of mutual obligations.

Though these systems varied among different land groups, they each harnessed the principles of food production with reciprocity, ensuring that people, places, flora, and fauna maintained a balanced custodianship over one another.

Over time, our Ancestors meticulously crafted these social blueprints, some refer to as social superstructures, to manage communication, behaviour, relationships and to process conflict ensuring the sustainability of land and language groups.

These approaches, deeply embedded in the fabric of their societies, fostered a continuity that enabled them to endure even colonisation's relentless attempts to extinguish their presence. Through these persistent ancient systems, the Ancestors safeguarded the survival and vitality of our cultures, preserving their essence against the tides of change.

In times of past fears, our Ancestors foresaw the peril of endless conflict and the loss of peace, harmony, and balance. They understood that without the virtues arising from their social arrangements, we might succumb to our own temptations and desires, endangering our very survival. To safeguard our future, they meticulously crafted laws and wove them into the fabric of our landscapes, anchoring us to Earth, our Mother. As her children, our duty is to realign ourselves with her wisdom, focusing intently on nurturing peace and reciprocity.

By honouring these ancient laws and fostering harmonious relationships with each other and the land, we uphold the legacy of our Ancestors and ensure the flourishing of all life that connects us to our shared home.

Alejandro Pastori - Uruguay

Alejandro Pastori is an Adjunct Professor of International Public Law at the University of the Republic in Montevideo, Uruguay. He acts as a legal advisor and consultant to international organizations and the Ministry of Foreign Affairs of his country. He is a member of the Board of the Uruguayan Council for International Relations, a Member of the Uruguayan national group of the Permanent Court of Arbitration, and a Rotary Peace Fellow.

Peace: A Balance of Interests and a New Institutional Framework

Like the idea of justice in law, peace is an ideal to strive for, knowing in advance that it will never be completely achieved.

In national communities, the more prosperity and justice and the less inequality, the greater the chances that society will not resort to violence. Unfortunately, at the international level, the struggle of States for their global positioning lacks the ideals of justice and equality and it is managed by interests, more linked to the ideas of prosperity and power.

International rules seek to avoid conflicts or to protect individual rights, but they do not always succeed.

Global peace can therefore only be achieved when the equation of interests is balanced, and the cost of conflict is higher than that of the non-conflict status quo.

The possibilities for global peace will depend on the management of this balance, and all the factors that make it up (commercial, military, financial, religious, cultural, etc.). To this end, the structuring of a more efficient universal negotiation framework than the one currently existing is the only way to stop the unilateralism of actions and to create negotiation environments where this balance can be achieved to ensure a relatively lasting peace.

Kant's idea of a perpetual peace is that it is only possible in moments, a bit like happiness.

For that very reason let's create mechanisms that are appropriate to make it last as long as possible and forget about the existing mechanism that was built in 1945 for a post-WWII scenario.

We don't need to wait for WWIII for that.

Chapter Eight: Enough Already

*Never be afraid to raise your voice for honesty and truth and
compassion against injustice and lying and greed. If people all over
the world... would do this, it would change the earth.*
- William Faulkner

My peacebuilding roots were formed during the era of the 1970s anti-war and pro-women's rights movements in North America. Whether it was marches and sit-ins to protest war, or occupying the university president's office to protest student tuition increases, or blockades to protest the forestry practices of big corporations, we raised our voices, used our feet, and, as Sally Armstrong says, grabbed a few headlines.

Activism has, for the most part, made way for advocacy in my peacebuilding work. But not completely. In the past eight years, I have organized women's marches, walked alongside my Muslim neighbours protesting the violence their community has suffered in our country, spoken at protests highlighting the genocides and femicides happening in our world, and joined the #womenseriously movement started by Irene Santiago and colleagues.

I even took a stab at leadership through engaging in politics.

Activists, advocates and leaders: we need them all to change the system; to tackle the determinants of violence and the policies that sustain them.

Activists know the power of action. At the beginning of this book is a quote from Rebecca Solnit about hope. She challenges us to wield hope like an axe and break down the doors. I believe that if we didn't have hope, we wouldn't act.

The work of activists informs advocates on how to move the message on to the larger community, into dialogue among leaders, and ultimately to the goal: change.

"Enough already" faces the reality and truth of our collective situation. In the absence of peace-motivated leadership, the activists and advocates among us must speak up, organize and be a visible and persistent community.

The contributors to this chapter inspire us to stand for, stand up, stand beside, and not stand still, to speak up and to give voice to the experiences, knowledge, and passion of the peacebuilders. They encourage us to refuse to accept the status quo, call out corruption, advocate for transformational change in how we allocate public funds, and demand that leaders support peace practices rather than those of war. When leaders equate militarization with security, we need to call them out and challenge them to think about security in a different way: in a peacebuilding way.

We need to raise our voices, hold on to the vision of a different future for our planet, and establish leadership that reflects a future that is informed by the lessons we have learned. Because truly – enough already!

There may be times when we are powerless to prevent injustice, but
there must never be a time when we fail to protest.
\- Elie Wiesel.

Deborah Ellis - Canada

Deborah Ellis is the author of twenty-plus books for young people, focussing on children and war in its many forms.

Enough Already!

"We are not so mad as to think we shall create a world in which murder will not occur. We are fighting for a world in which murder will no longer be legal."

To this wonderful statement by Albert Camus, I would add that we want a world where war is no longer profitable. Why should someone be allowed to get rich off the murder of others? If arms manufacturers can no longer make money from making weapons, they'll stop making them.

Enough already. We have learned all we can from killing each other. Let's learn something new.

Leo Broderick - Canada

Leo Broderick is a passionate activist for social and environmental justice with a deep understanding of global and local issues. In addition to his distinguished career as an educator, he consistently proves how ordinary citizens can have an influence to make the world a safer, fairer place. He has been a member and President of the Board of Directors for the Council of Canadians, Canada's leading social action organization with more than 50 chapters across Canada.
www.canadians.org

The Power of Protest

What are global citizens to do about the many violent conflicts around the world? It's daunting, and seems hopeless at times, especially for peace activists. It's distressing that world military expenditure increased for the ninth consecutive year reaching a total of $2443 billion in 2023.

Our world is burning and flooding, and instead of coming together to save planet earth, we continue to be busy building nuclear submarines, nuclear arms, hypersonic missiles and other weapons of doom and destruction. Military corporations are at the heart of the problem - one corporation like U.S.-based Lockheed Martin makes close to $68 billion a year.

A reality we must come to acknowledge is that the world's military corporations, and they are increasing in numbers, depend on wars, the preparation for wars, and constantly instilling the fear of wars in the vast majority of the world's population.

That's how they stay in business, and that's how they see their profits surge and surge. And the result of this global militarization is the horrendous cost to civilians and societies.

In order for wars to occur, the concept of 'dehumanization' is added to the mix. Dehumanization is the act of regarding, representing, or treating a person 'less than human.' The dehumanization of the 'enemy' is what sustains wars. Killing the enemy becomes easy, and supposedly someone's world becomes safer. Killing one's way to peace is such a contradiction - yet it is the corporate capitalist model approach made popular in cultures by political and military leaders.

So, what do peacemakers do when faced with these dilemmas? We can demand through local and international peace groups that global military spending be reduced significantly, and that these public funds be redirected to meet true human needs.

We can call out governments, political leaders, institutions, and individuals who use dehumanizing language against any group or individual. We can work to ensure that human rights and the rights to peace and security are respected. And we can through public education address the root causes of conflict which are economic and social injustices, discrimination, and oppression. But equally important we can join local and global peaceful protests which can have a powerful and lasting impact in shaping the world as a fairer, freer and a more peaceful place for all humanity.

Lisa Linda Natividad is a Professor of social work and Chamoru studies at the University of Guam. She also manages a private behavioural health practice. She is a founding member of the Pacific Indigenous Women's Network and I Hagan Famalao'an Guahan. She currently serves on the board of the International Peace Bureau and the Guahan Coalition for Peace and Justice. She lives on Guahan in the village of Inalåhan with her son, Atdao-mami.

Peace Through the Lens of Love and Compassion

The concept of peace can be abstract and aspirational. It is often relegated to being a dream of the naïve and innocent. In modern times, wherein interstate wars are being fought and a country whose economic rise has the current Empire threatened, society has normalized militarization.

In 2024, the United States' military spending totaled nearly $900 billion. It was spent on war preparation, the modernization of weaponry, and the development and maintenance of nearly 1,000 foreign military bases.

Imagine if these funds were used to promote genuine security.

Aligned with the United Nations' concept of human security, genuine security is characterized by our physical environment sustaining human and natural life; peoples' basic needs for food, clothing, shelter, health care, and education being assured;

honoring and respecting human dignity and cultural identities; and protecting people and the natural environment from avoidable harm. If this were the case, communities would maximize their potential and thrive.

When young children experience conflict among their peers, parental figures typically teach them to take responsibility for their actions and apologize when one has harmed the other. The result of this process is conflict resolution, and the children return to play learning to set boundaries, respect each other's differences, and work together. Why is it that when countries experience conflict, violence is justified?

To achieve peace, we must look through the lens of love and compassion.

We cannot allow ourselves to accept war and the suffering that comes with it as a normal part of the human experience. Violence in all shapes and forms must be removed from the repertoire of peacebuilding. We must commit to the fundamental notion that there is no circumstance that justifies violence and rise to the highest station of our being to achieve peace.

Let us remember the wisdom of the peaceful movements for justice such as those led by Gandhi and Dr. Martin Luther

King, Jr. Employing the power of diplomacy and compassion as we engage global tensions creates the opportunity to achieve peace. As peacebuilders, let us return to the fundamental lessons of conflict resolution taught to us as children.

May we always aspire for peace by learning to respect and love each other

Regina M. Mwendwa - Kenya

Regina Mwendwa is a seasoned peacebuilding practitioner focusing on community-led peacebuilding, women, youth, peace and security, prevention of violent extremism, and policy. She holds an MA in Peace, Conflict and Development from the University of Bradford, UK and a BA in Development Communication from St Paul's University, Kenya. She is a member of FemWise, the African Union arm of women in conflict prevention. She works with the National Cohesion and Integration Commission in Kenya and is a Rotary Peace Fellow (RPF) and board member of the RPF Alumni Association.

End Corruption Now: A Threat to Peace and Stability

I know this may sound cliché but allow me to build my case using the Institute for Peace and Economics study, which identifies low levels of corruption as one of the eight pillars of positive peace.

The study notes that "in societies with high levels of corruption, resources are inefficiently allocated, often leading to a lack of funding for essential services and civil unrest."

In recent years, we've seen how bad governance, particularly corruption, has led to social friction, the breakdown of services, and civil unrest—from West Africa to East Africa to Bangladesh.

The Gen Z protests in Kenya, my country, are a powerful example of young people demanding good governance. While these protests began with the rejection of the Finance Bill 2024, which introduced new taxes, the underlying cause of their anger was corruption.

Gen Z reached a breaking point, no longer willing to tolerate the blatant display of stolen wealth and opulence by senior public figures and politicians, along with the misallocation of public funds to the first family offices and political appointees. They took to the streets, demanding that the president fire his entire corrupt cabinet. "Our parents are suffering from high living costs and a lack of a good healthcare system, while our politicians enjoy lavish lifestyles," one youth decried.

In response to the Gen Z protests, which resulted in the loss of lives and destruction of property, the president not only dropped the Finance Bill 2024 but also dismissed his entire cabinet, scrapped certain government offices, and pledged to cut wasteful spending by dissolving state firms and reducing the number of government advisors. A police chief also resigned in response to these demands.

While Kenya has not yet fully eradicated corruption—a fundamental threat to peace and stability—the Gen Z call to end it is a step in the right direction, an action that can be emulated to build peaceful communities.

Nobody need wait a single moment before starting to improve the world.
- Anne Frank

Dhruti Shah - England

Dhruti Shah was brought up in the peace-focused Jain faith. She is a British Rotary International Peace Fellow who studied at the Rotary Peace Centre at Chulalongkorn University in 2017. She is a freelance creative practitioner and journalist who believes that stories are a way of helping create a common bond when it comes to peace and conflict resolution.

Surfing the Waves of Peacebuilding

It's very easy to talk of peace. What's more difficult is taking action. When you hear the word peace or read it or whichever way you approach it, what is the image that comes to mind? A dove? The sea? An olive branch?

To a dispassionate observer the notion of peace can seem like a passive act – to have peace is to allow things to be, to have a stillness. Sounds serene right? That thought of inner peace where the worries and anxieties of the world around us don't burn our core.

But when you're still, that's when the status quo remains still too. And that's not always the best course of action.

Peace needs to be about compromise and an ever-shifting and evolving state where conversations and actions keep happening so that the different parties involved can keep moving forward and adapt as circumstances around us change.

Peace involves protest and standing up for injustice and a constant having to be alert to ensure that dominant parties stand up for those who are marginalised or under threat. Peace involves activity, open dialogue, and bringing a variety of voices to the table.

Often when you dig into peace you stir up trouble. And by taking action to bring forth peace, well, you're already breaking that status quo.

Get ready to surf those waves; follow the birds and plant those roots

Julie L. Cormack - Canada

Retired anthropologist, **Julie L. Cormack** is a member of WILPF Canada (Women's International League for Peace & Freedom), and VOW (Canadian Voice of Women for Peace/Nova Scotia Voice of Women for Peace). She regularly participates in the Wolfville Peace Vigil and local Friends meetings. She is a UN representative to New York for Servas International where her interest is nuclear disarmament. She is also a member of GAMIP (Global Alliance for Ministries & Infrastructures for Peace), an international community building cultures of peace and local ministries of peace in various countries.

Peace (is) not war; it is so much more

Peace is a journey - peace walks, peace marches, peace caravans　　*Are we there yet?*

Peace is an action – peace movements, peace camps, peacekeepers, pacifism

Peace is present / Peace is a presence　*Peace is part of our being; do we hear her calling?*

Peace is an emotion: Peace and quiet ~ Peace and happiness ~ Peace and joy ~ Peace of mind ~ Love and peace

Peace expressed in voice, music, art and culture has many forms: nonviolent communication, listening, trust, negotiation, diplomacy, mediation, peacebuilding

With peace comes hope, justice, freedom, equity, inclusion, and voice to those who have none

Peace is global - Paix, Pace, Hasîtî, शान्ति, Barış, 和平,　Мир, سلام, שלום, Papayatik

Peace embodies the Golden Rule – "Treat others the way you want to be treated" *Love thy neighbour*

Peace evokes connection, conversation, communication, cooperation, completeness

Peace is a way of life based on sensitivity, understanding, and unity

Ursula Franklin defined Peace as "the presence of justice and the absence of fear." We have the words, the ideas, the images.

Do we have the courage?

Sally Armstrong - Canada

Human rights activist, journalist and award-winning author **Sally Armstrong** has covered stories about women and girls in zones of conflict all over the world. She received the Amnesty International Canada Media Award in 2000, 2002, 2011 and again in 2017. She was named the Massey Lecturer for 2019. The lectures and book are titled *Power Shift: The Longest Revolution*. In 2020 she received the Lifetime Achievement Award from Women of Influence. Also, in 2020 she delivered the Judy LaMarsh Lecture at Victoria College/University of Toronto. She was a member of the International Women's Commission, a UN body that consists of 20 Palestinian women, 20 Israeli women and 12 internationals whose mandate was assisting with the path to peace in the Middle East. She is the recipient of eleven honorary doctorate degrees and one honorary diploma and is an Officer of the Order of Canada. *Outspoken: My Fight for Freedom and Human Rights in Afghanistan* by Sima Samar with Sally Armstrong was published in 2024.

Seeking Peace

The trouble with peace is that war gets all the attention. Even though war wrecks the economy, destroys health and has long-term consequences compared to peace that boosts the economy, improves health and increases well-being, it's war that gets our attention. Peace needs to find a way to grab headlines, make news, become a hot topic of conversation.

I have been covering war as a journalist for more than 30 years. In Africa, in Europe, in the Middle East and in Asia, I have been an eyewitness to the senseless destruction, the loss of life, the colossal waste of human resources and money and indeed the near destruction of civilization. I have seen the consequences of war and the rejection of peace.

There are no winners in war. Everyone loses in one way or another. Invariably the threads that weave the battle together are created by a small collection of greedy men who seek power. Take Iran – I don't believe the people of Iran give a hoot about the people of Israel and by the same token I don't believe the people of Israel spare a thought for the people of Iran. This is an ongoing conflict created by leaders who seek personal aggrandizement through power and land and the subservience of the people. It is never about serving their people or improving the economy or making a better country.

In almost every zone of conflict, the rejection of peace comes at a terrible cost to the citizens. My experience tells me that the people on one side do not hate the people on the other; they often lived together, worked together, and married each other. It's leaders who seek war and civilians who beg for peace.

It's the barriers to peace that stop ordinary people from refusing war. Those barriers are so firmly entrenched they have eluded peace for centuries. The barriers come in the form of threats – those people will destroy your family (or your crop or your house). They come in the form of lies – that religion (or tribe or culture) is going to wipe you out. They come in the form of empty promises – we will defeat them and everything you ever wanted will be yours. As history has proven – those are false barriers.

It's time for peacebuilders to take the barriers down, to call out and name the warriors for what they are – greedy men seeking power. Religion is about your relationship to God or Allah; it's not a cover for misogyny. Land claims are settled in courts, not on battlefields. Women and men are equal – they are not the tools of political opportunism. Countries belong to citizens not to self-absorbed leaders who keep the war kettle boiling.

Speak your peace. Others will listen.

Epilogue

they say we are at war

i think we are falling in love

with the human race

~ John Paul Lederach
from an 'Unfolding Poem' for the Moment We're In[15]

---

[15] https://onbeing.org/blog/an-unfolding-poem-for-the-moment-were-in/

Acknowledgements

This book started as an idea, as all books do; an idea that arose from an antsy feeling of needing to do something in the face of all of the bad news coming at me. The first person I sought advice from was my friend, Todd MacLean, the editor of the wonderful Global Chorus. What did he think of a similar book, one to tackle the question of peace in our world? He responded, "Exactly what we need today, and you are the person to do it!" My first thanks go to Todd for believing in the project, and believing in me, and for the advice he has given me along this journey.

Global Voices for Peace would not have been possible without the strength of relationships developed within the Rotary peacebuilding community. The response from my fellow Rotary Peace Fellows has been enthusiastic, generous, and heartwarming. I am immensely grateful to the Rotary Foundation for the opportunity to study Peace and Conflict at the Rotary Peace Centre in Bangkok, and all of the Rotarians and Rotary clubs to whom I have presented and who have supported projects such as this.

Each reflection gives us a glimpse into the hard work of dedicated peacebuilders, and I want to extend my gratitude to each one of you – your work is invaluable. Thank you for trusting me to share your thoughts and for introducing me to other peacebuilders throughout the world.

There have been several people I have turned to for advice along the way – my son, Benton Hartley, for his writing and book business knowledge, Ron Patterson for his editing skills and geopolitical acumen, and Sharon McKay for her knowledge about the book industry.

I am sure this book would not have been realized without the practical, organizational, and technological skills that my partner and husband, Chris Hartley. Thank you for your love and dedication to both me and the project.

Index of Contributors

231